LIGHT
COLOR
TEXTURE

The work of **MDSA** MDSzerbaty Associates Architecture

LIGHT COLOR TEXTURE

images
Publishing

Contents

8 Preface

12 Introduction

16 Materiality: Light, Color, Texture

20 Letting in the Light
The Sixth Avenue Elementary School PS340M

34 Inspired by the Landscape
Morning Sky House, Guest House and Stable

54 Opening Up Connections
Cornell ILR 34th Street Conference Center

64 The Inherent Quality of Materials

68 Transparency in the Park
Mosaic Pre-K Center

86 Light and Shadow and the Responsibility of the Joint

90 Shadow Play
Pre-K Center K613

100 A Box in the Park
NYCHA Superstorm Sandy Resiliency & Renewal Program at LaGuardia Houses

108 Rising Above
NYCHA: Child Care and Community Center at Redfern Houses Complex

120 Origins of a Design Philosophy

124 Changing Face
Universal Physical Education Gyms

132 Bayside Blue
Ocean Bay Apartment (Bayside) Sandy Resiliency & Renewal Program

146 Early Childhood Education and the Influence of Color

150 Respecting the Original
Richard Rodgers School PS96X Addition

160 Peripheral Vision

164 Firm History

172 Project Credits

174 Acknowledgments

Preface

For this monograph, we at MDSzerbaty Associates Architecture (MDSA) present an in-depth examination of a smaller number of the firm's projects, rather than presenting an overview of a large number of its completed works. Looking closely at the details, materials, and play of natural light across our projects gives a clear understanding of how we approach design, execution, and longevity in our work. Showcasing our projects this way is a powerful approach, as it extends the projects through time and shows a level of consistent thinking as the work evolves. To demonstrate this idea, the monograph will look at how the firm conceptualizes its work through sketches and diagrams, analyzes projects to reinforce the idea through their development, and considers the use of materials as elements that define a space or surface.

An enclosure and interior surface are defined by the material chosen, along with its qualities of texture and color. Tactility can also be important. As materials age, they take on different qualities. The effects of natural sunlight, wind, and rain are experienced over time. The change of season throughout each year is a constantly repeating, but ever unique, event.

Many of these close observations come from maintaining a close connection with the work we do beyond its design and construction, by revisiting or even living there, "feeling" the life of photographic images over time, seeing the transformations that occur with age. Many cannot understand this without having such exposure, nor does it occur to someone who experiences these changes on all projects. The single-family house is the most intimate example, but as the firm's projects are mostly concentrated within a geographic region, an occasional revisit of several projects is common over a period of many years. Designed with permanence in mind, and well maintained over long periods of time, the buildings can be appreciated for their clarity, and how the imaginative use of materials and their detailing transform themselves, and allow the daily users an appreciation of the nuances that take place.

The examples of work in this monograph demonstrate how the Architect—the Firm—intentionally deliberates and considers materials, colors, and textures in thinking about the execution of a project. This evolutionary process is evidenced across the body of work presented here.

Michael D. Szerbaty

Introduction

The projects presented in this monograph represent a wide range of type, scale, and context. They also vary widely in clientele, from the intimacy of a private residence, to public buildings, to structures that are not accessible to the public and can only be experienced from outside. They share a common ideal: the sophisticated and refined consideration of light, texture, and color, shown through detailing and execution.

Ours is a process of "Imagination through Collaboration." MDSA gains strength from the diversity of our work. The firm believes that designing and constructing projects that vary in scale, scope, and budget enable a cross-fertilization of ideas used in concept, material usage, and detailing, allowing us to better explore new approaches to how people live, learn, work, and experience buildings. The variety of project types provides us with exposure to differing approaches and priorities among clients and users. Dialogue enables our imagination.

Our solutions are not preconceived design ideas; instead, they mature through a process of creative collaboration and exploration of how spatial and material solutions can respond to client needs. It is the firm's belief that each project requires a nuanced approach to consistently yield innovative and responsive solutions to complex design issues.

Our approach is to explore the hierarchies and interplay inherent in any given program and site. We generate inventive spatial solutions through the interaction of these program and site elements, with results that achieve richness through the light, (infra)structure, and materials that shape them. MDSA thoughtfully weaves together pragmatic, creative, and economic concerns into good buildings. We excel in an environment that encourages multiple perspectives and varying commentary, which stimulates our drive to make better architecture.

We create buildings and interiors with presence—that have an integrity that speaks quietly and directly. Our spaces reveal themselves in layers to offer a richness of experience that continues over time. We bring an intensity of focus that extends from the overall concept to the fine details, energizing even routine spaces. That consistency means the entire project is responsive to the client's needs and goals, and how the user experiences the spaces.

Of paramount importance to our design work is the careful composition and use of materials. We use materials not only for their sensory qualities of texture and color, but also inventively integrate them with adjacent elements with technical precision and detailing that yields a refined and sophisticated appearance. Our work carefully considers texture, color, and natural light. We seek to explore the inherent qualities of materials in their use and relationship in ways that may, at first sight, seem disparate with adjacent elements, but ultimately reveals a sophisticated and refined approach. We particularly pride ourselves upon technical precision, as well as knowledge and innovation in construction techniques and the assembly of building systems.

Whether it is through an open space, an unexpected jolt of texture or color, a plan that provides a sense of place, or a welcome wash of daylight, we infuse each space with vibrancy. It is with this insight and dedication that the work of the firm is pursued for its clients.

Materiality: Light, Color, Texture

MDSA's use of materials is not only for their sensory qualities of texture and color, but also to inventively integrate them with adjacent elements with technical precision and detailing that yields a refined and sophisticated appearance. Seemingly disparate relationships become harmonic and reliant on one another. The juxtaposed materials remain distinct in their own capacity and quality. It is the detailing within and between that permits their coexistence.

Daylighting refers to the capacity for surfaces and spaces to be daylit. The careful consideration of spatial form regarding how light travels, settles, and diffuses within and between spaces and onto materials is something generalized when design and planning concepts are developed. The cardinal points of north, south, east, and west are understood and form part of the thought process in any intelligent design. Coupled with other site issues such as view, topography, and environmental concerns, these can and should be drivers in the design, formed around the program of the building.

The sun sets its own course across any site and building form that, though a constant repeat over the course of a year, dramatically affects the reading of a space through direct and indirect light, shadow, and near darkness. The precision with which a design considers the effect of light over time gives a bonus to a project. The use of physical and visual connections is increased by a sense of environmental awareness, which in turn creates a more legible place. Better connected spaces increase the possibilities of how a space can be used; promotes growth in different ways; and supports a better and increased use of the building.

As the plan and section develop, these concerns start to penetrate the building and site. The use of double-height spaces, voids, glass, openings, and light control technologies are all techniques that enhance the quality of space.

Clockwise from top left: The shadow box behind the glass; A mosaic of color and texture made by light; Morning light in layers of transparency; The exaggeration of dark and light and color; Weathering Steel Panels—aged five years, with a southern orientation in a dry climate

At a point, the surfaces and spaces that have been formed become defined by materials. The basic material palette—glass (transparent and opaque/translucent), stone/tile, precast concrete, wood, metal, solid surface, plaster/sheetrock—has longevity and durability, and, most importantly, consideration in how they absorb and react to the local light in a given orientation relative to their own texture. Some materials such as precast concrete are molded to respond to light through shadow and depth perception; they reflect the light. Others (like glass) look to create layers of transparency and visual depth through a play of translucency and opacity. The light can be compressed or the depth of the space beyond can be captured in layers of transparency. In contrast, there are other materials (such as weathering steel) that completely absorb light through the pitted texture they develop over time.

It is important to note here that it is the nature of the material itself that yields such—at times—phenomenal attributes. It needs no intervention on the part of the Architect to display its qualities, only for the Architect to appreciate those qualities that exist inherently when considering the composition. The Architect cannot/should not be a decorator bending things to their will. At the same time, such characteristics come to life only through a deliberate and thoughtful application in the design process, followed through in the details. Memory serves to create an indelible mark of success in something that previously existed only as lines on paper.

Clockwise from top left: Texture versus color; The nature of the material and its reflections; A simple surface alive in light; Reading texture through shadows; Subtle but distinct are the colors and textures

The Sixth Avenue Elementary School PS340M

Manhattan, New York

Letting in the Light

In a dense, high-rise urban environment, multistory school buildings have a unique presence. Such schools rarely find themselves as stand-alone buildings; instead, they are part of a mixed-use program inside a new development or a major renovation. Located at the bustling corner of the Avenue of Americas and 17th Street in Manhattan, the 95,000-square-foot PS340M involved converting the lower six floors and cellar of a 14-story building into a richly programmed Pre-K through Grade 5 school that serves 518 students. The original building, constructed as recently as 1989, served as a hospital. By condominium agreement the school exists at the lower floors while hospital administrative facilities remain at the top levels.

Within New York's tight urban environment, the challenge was to design a vibrant and protective learning environment for the students while still connecting with the energy of the city. Introducing natural light is always an issue and with the building located along the Avenue, high-rise structures dominate the fabric. Luckily the building had setbacks and a rear yard, which with careful planning could permit penetration of natural light deep into the school and rather dynamic views from inside the building to the Chelsea neighborhood outside.

EXIT
PS340

The main idea for the planning of the vertical school rested upon how to penetrate the building façade to gather as much natural light as possible. The quality of light changes dramatically over the course of the year as the sun yields to shadows created by surrounding buildings. We chose to carve out the inside of the building to allow the light to penetrate a series of double-height spaces linking the program together.

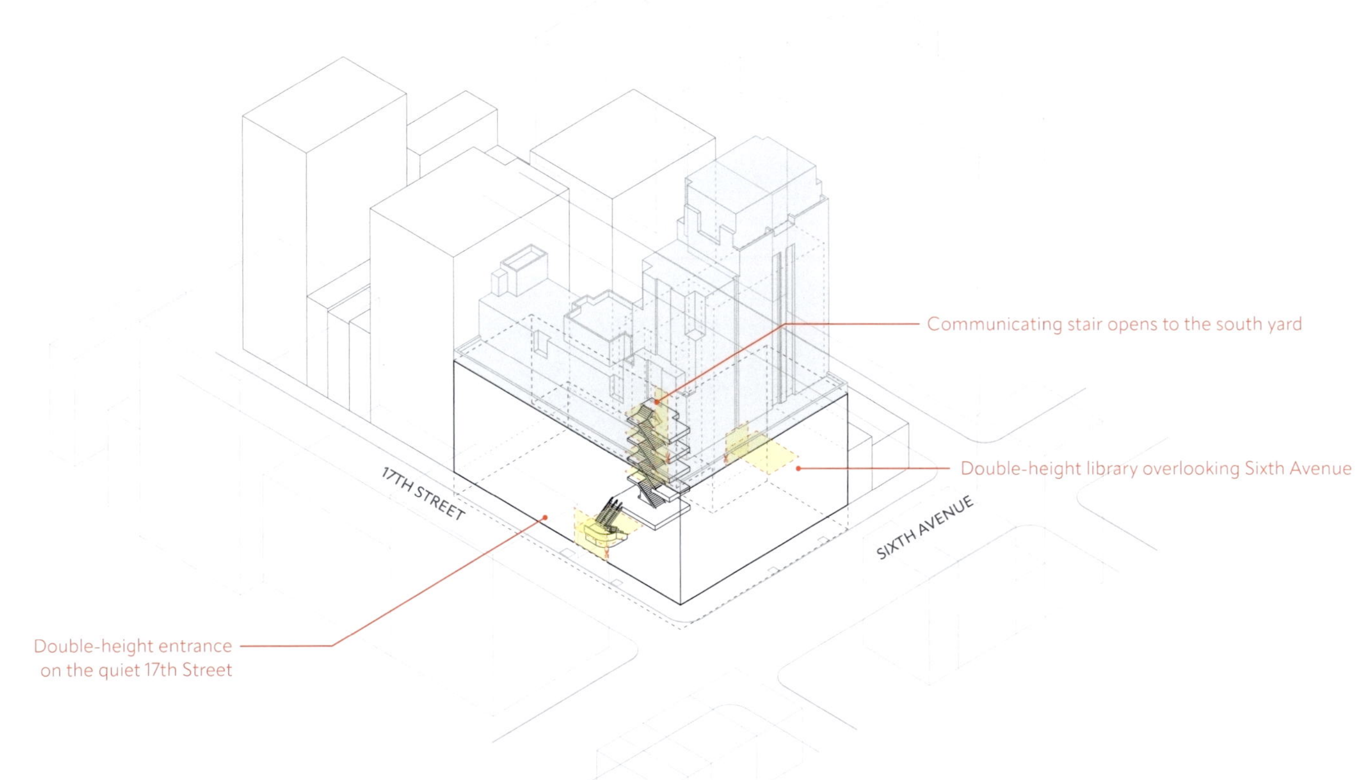

New openings and communicating stair result in visual connections and spreads the light inside

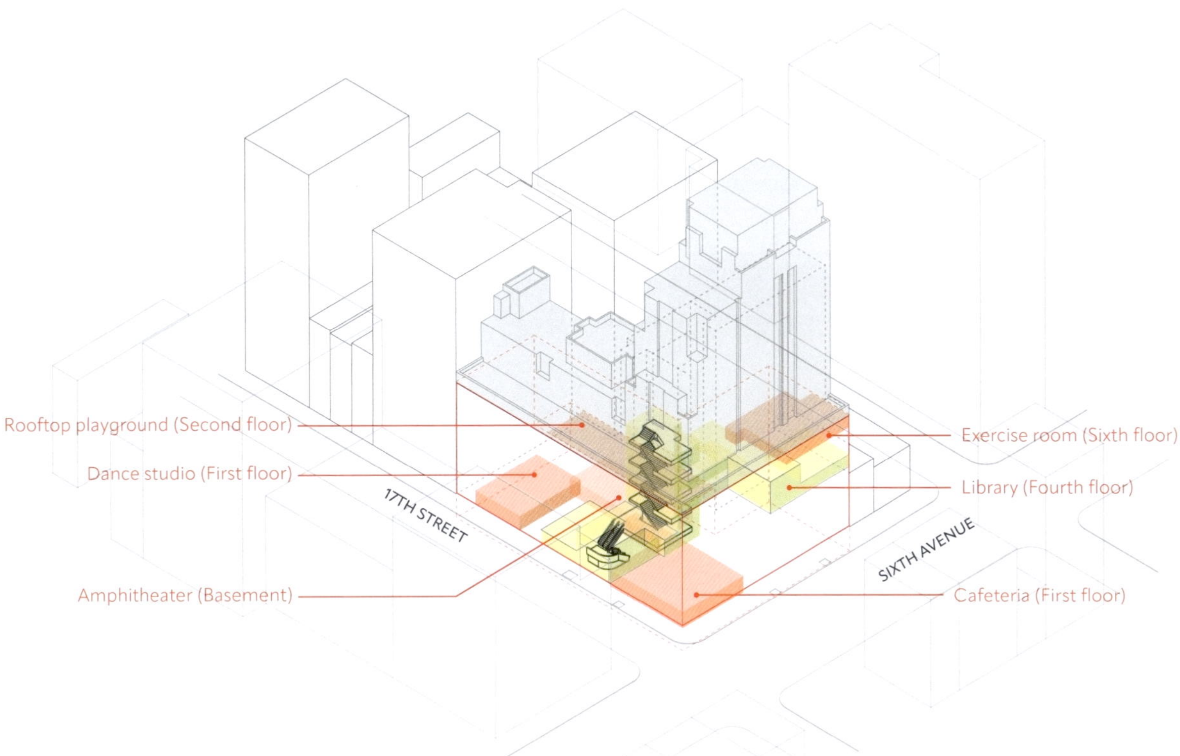

Special program spaces are dispersed along the space containing the communicating stair

Exercising

The school entrance faces north to 17th Street, open and inviting with an identifiable street presence. Passersby can look through a new, large glass surface to see the lobby's main monumental stair element. The wall of the south-facing rear yard of the building has a large section removed, replaced by a glass curtain wall to bring much-needed natural light deep into the interior, something lacking in the original punched-window building. Light and street level views are introduced at the north-facing entry, contrasting it with direct sunlight and views to the south. The main stair at the street level (joining levels 1 and 2) is presented as a solid occupying the carved double-height lobby space. It is a major gathering area for students and parents during arrival and dismissal. In direct contrast, the communicating stair shifts to the rear of the building to connect floor levels 2-6 and is made open and transparent, filtering light from the new curtain wall as it continues to the upper levels. The plan and sectional shift allow for a variety of visual experiences, and an infusion of natural light and views of the city, while unifying the spaces of the school from top to bottom.

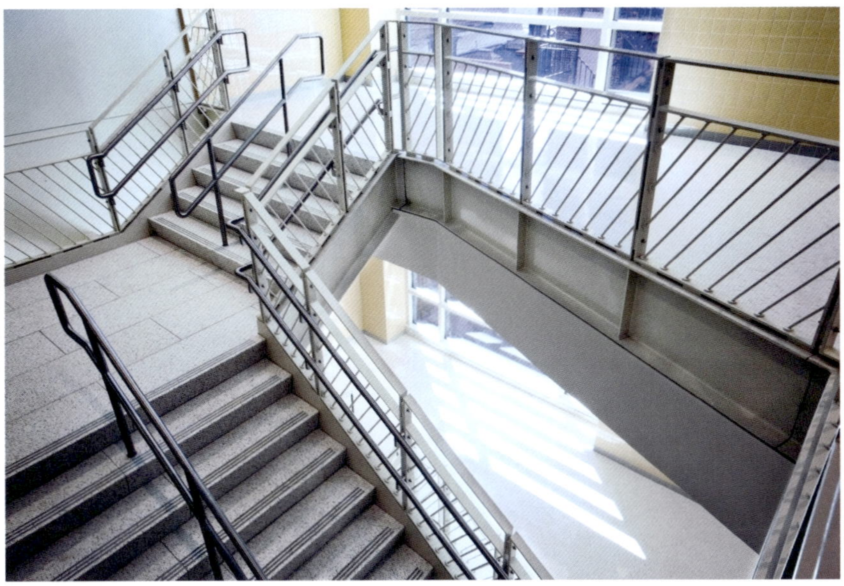

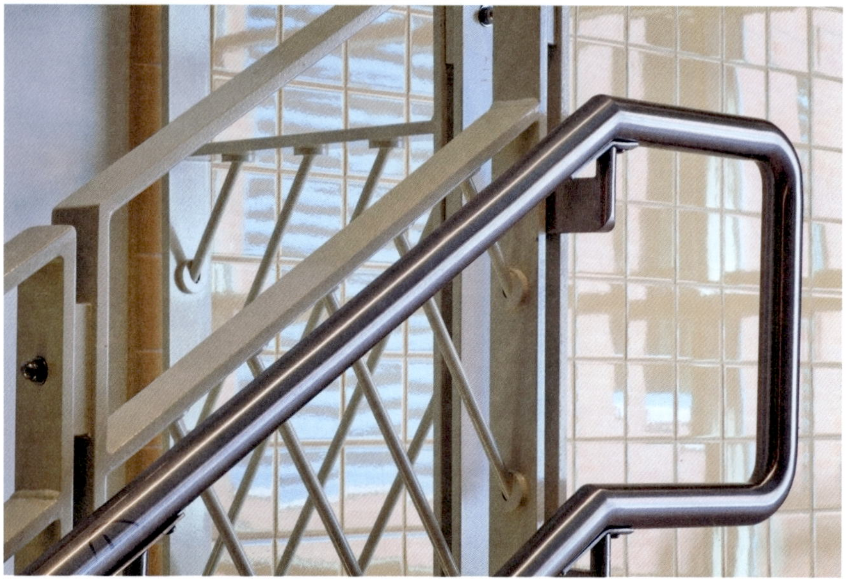

There is a prevalent color and material theme that ties together the vertical nature of the school: yellow and black solids with glass walls and metal railings. This treatment is conceived to contrast and play against the more animated interior palette of interwoven colors of hallways and classrooms. Commissioned via the Percent for Art Program, the artist Odili Donald Odila designed a colorful signature graphic at the main lobby wall visible from the street, codifying the internal palette of the school.

The distribution of program for the school is such that every other floor contains a major communal space—lobby/cafeteria, admin/rooftop play yard, library, exercise room—that are created by carving openings in the floor to create double-height spaces. The Sixth Avenue Elementary School includes 21 new classrooms arranged along the quieter 17th Street side of the building. Specialized instructional areas for art, music, science, and a multipurpose room look over the Avenue of the Americas from the upper floors.

The cellar level has as a bonus a small lecture hall available for community use. A community room is on the second floor adjacent to the double-height main lobby, the same level as the administrative areas. The street façade was modified to incorporate a new entry vestibule. The original loading dock became the dance studio. In addition to the main entrance, the ground floor contains the cafeteria and dance studio, which are enclosed with transparent glass partitions that visually connect the entire floor.

The project's complexity, with the inherent conditions of the existing multitenant building, its orientation and massing required innovative solutions to create a school that is invigorating, inviting, and open.

Morning Sky House, Guest House and Stable

Cottonwood, Arizona

Inspired by the Landscape

The "big sky" of the desert Southwest gives sunlight a unique crispness and clarity, rendering amazing colors and shadows on the rocks and vegetation that shape the topography. It is this landscape that attracted the architect and his wife several years ago to the Verde Valley, just south of Sedona.

Located two hours north of Phoenix in the foothills of Mingus Mountain, the steeply sloping site has expansive views to the Verde Valley, Red Rock country of Sedona, and to San Francisco Peaks over 50 miles away. The slope orientation works perfectly with the spectacular panorama to the north, setting up a strategy of planning the project as a series of separate elements rising and falling with the topography, connected by a series of terraces and paths.

The house is nestled into the land at the high end of the 12-acre site. Its main entry is arrived at through a series of terraces and steps carved into the hill, constantly reorienting you to present varying views.

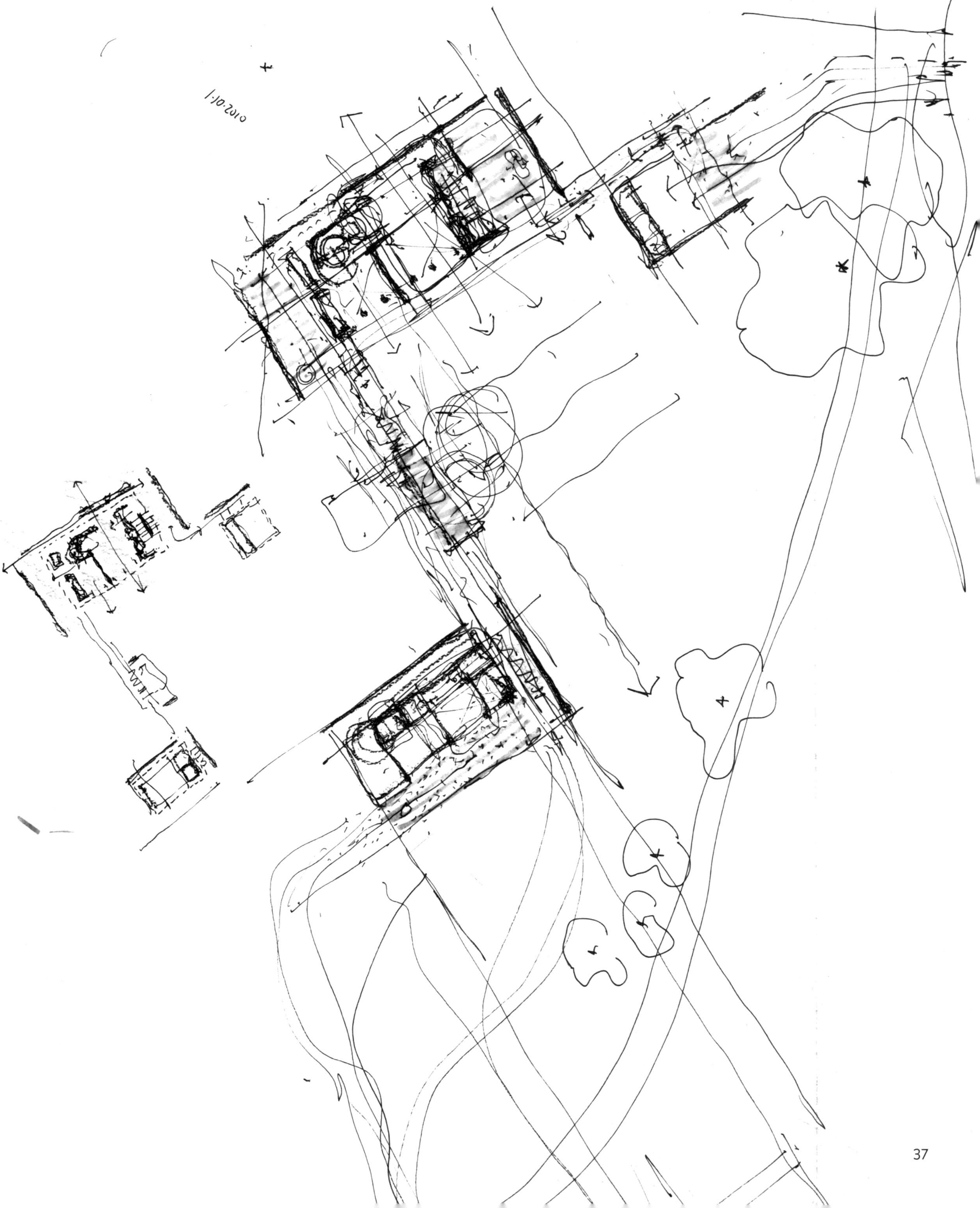
1-10-2010

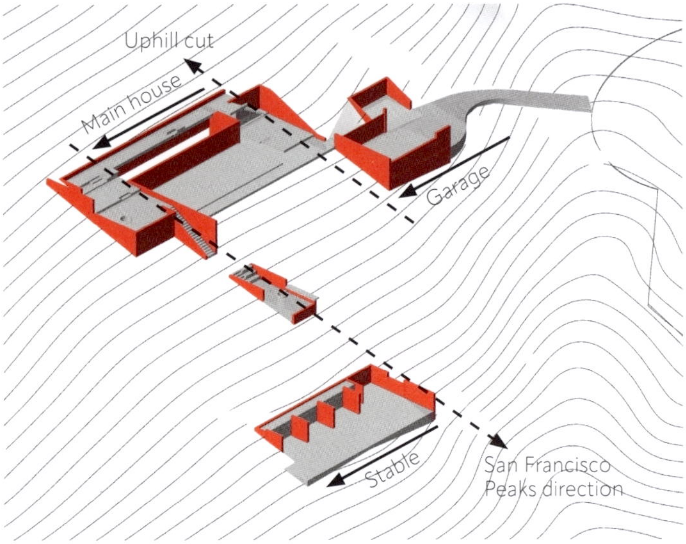

Cutting, carving, and filling voids in the natural landscape

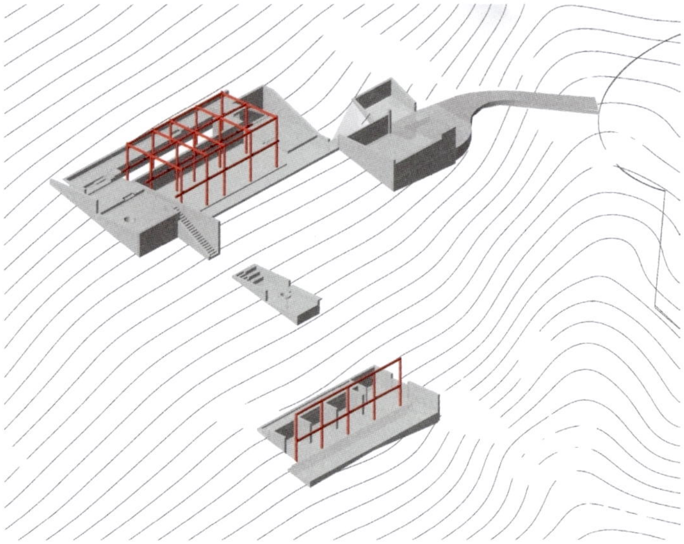

Post-and-beam structure inserted into the excavation

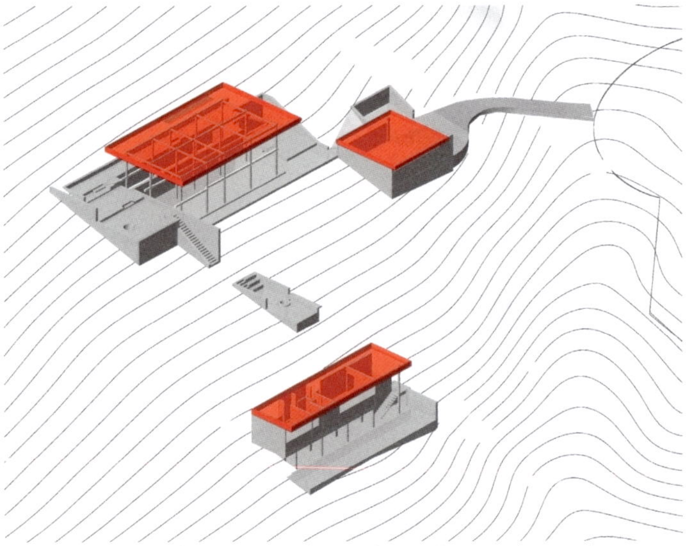

Each orientation of the main and guest house has overhangs whose dimension is determined in order to maximize sun exposure to the inside in the winter and provide shade in the summer

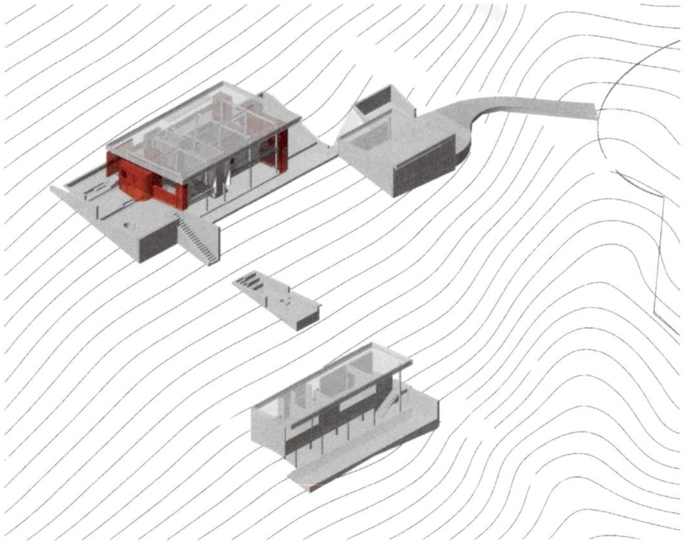

The solids floating within the free plan

First-floor plan

Ground floor plan

The 2,800-square-foot house is on two levels. An open plan characterizes the main house's upper level, with living, dining, and kitchen areas, a powder room and a master bedroom and bath. The main floor comprises a transparent space of living areas, while a more solid volume of playful forms define the private spaces. The upper level affords views not only to the valley below, but also to the mountain behind it forming the backdrop for the site.

The lower floor is cut into the land with windows facing north. A sky-lit open stair connects to this level, which includes a family area and study, a guest bedroom and laundry, mechanical, and storage spaces.

Dropping down the property, the horse stable and guest house volume is similarly carved into the slope, with the 750-square-foot studio floating on piers over the landscape and three-stall stable. It has an open kitchen with dining counter and living area. Down the hall is a bedroom and bathroom, flanked by closets.

Horses can roam a large portion of the property, which has fairly dense flora typical of the high desert—scrub oak, cacti, juniper, and cottonwood—and includes a wash with a spring that flows during the wet season.

The house, incorporating earth-tone colors and natural materials such as mahogany windows, Jatoba cherry and bluestone flooring, and a Douglas fir post-and-beam structure, is meant to disappear into the landscape. The large glass surfaces provide transparency, connecting inside to outside with a specific focus to views in each direction. Overhangs, whose dimensions are calculated from solar angles at each orientation, maximize sun exposure in the winter and provide shade in the summer.

The design of the house takes cues from the study of American Indian ruins, complexes constructed throughout the desert Southwest beginning in the tenth century. Cutting, carving, and filling voids of the natural landscape, these structures were molded with materials available, namely rocks and timbers. Orientation was planned considering command of the site and respect for the power of the sun. The intersecting geometries of the structures—squares, circles, and rectangles—result in dynamic webs of woven grids generated by this "scratching of the earth."

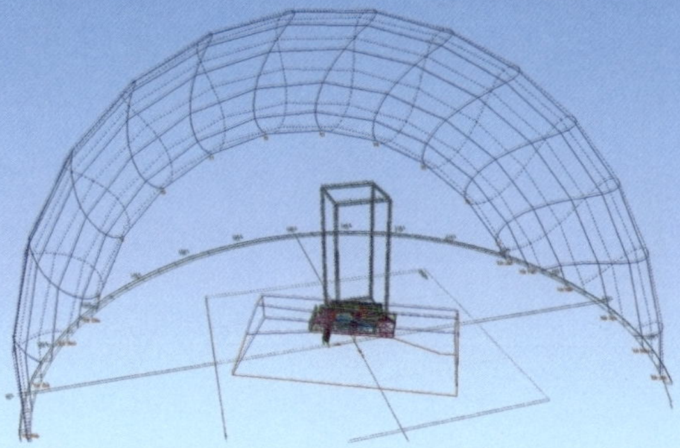

The Morning Sky house, guest house, and stable explores the meaning of such geometry overlaid on the spectacular natural landscape of the Verde Valley.

Cornell ILR 34th Street Conference Center

Manhattan, New York

Opening Up Connections

This modest project involved the reconfiguring and resequencing of spaces in the ILR School's 11,000-square-foot conference and continuing education center. The facility is located on the eighth floor of a typical mid-twentieth-century high-rise office building in mid-town Manhattan, New York City. The design renovated the facility's reception area, break room, and the resource library, with cosmetic upgrades to the rest of the floor, including furnishings.

By simply demolishing a number of interior partition walls within the area of the elevator lobby, the project was able to expand and create free-flowing connections between program spaces, in the long and short direction of the plan. Previously containing a dated library room with shelves of books, the proposed program aimed to reduce the amount of space devoted to housing physical media by 75 percent. This enabled the plan to be opened up with transparent connections to other areas. A new Resource Room was made, reflecting contemporary standards for a technology intensive and networked university library space.

Spaces are now open and visually transparent. A variety of glass partition elements permit greater visibility between interior spaces and allow natural light into the center of the plan. The multiuse nature of the instructional spaces, including the inherent flexibility of the furnishing and lighting systems, allows the new center to service a small seminar or workshop, as well as a large assembly for a symposium.

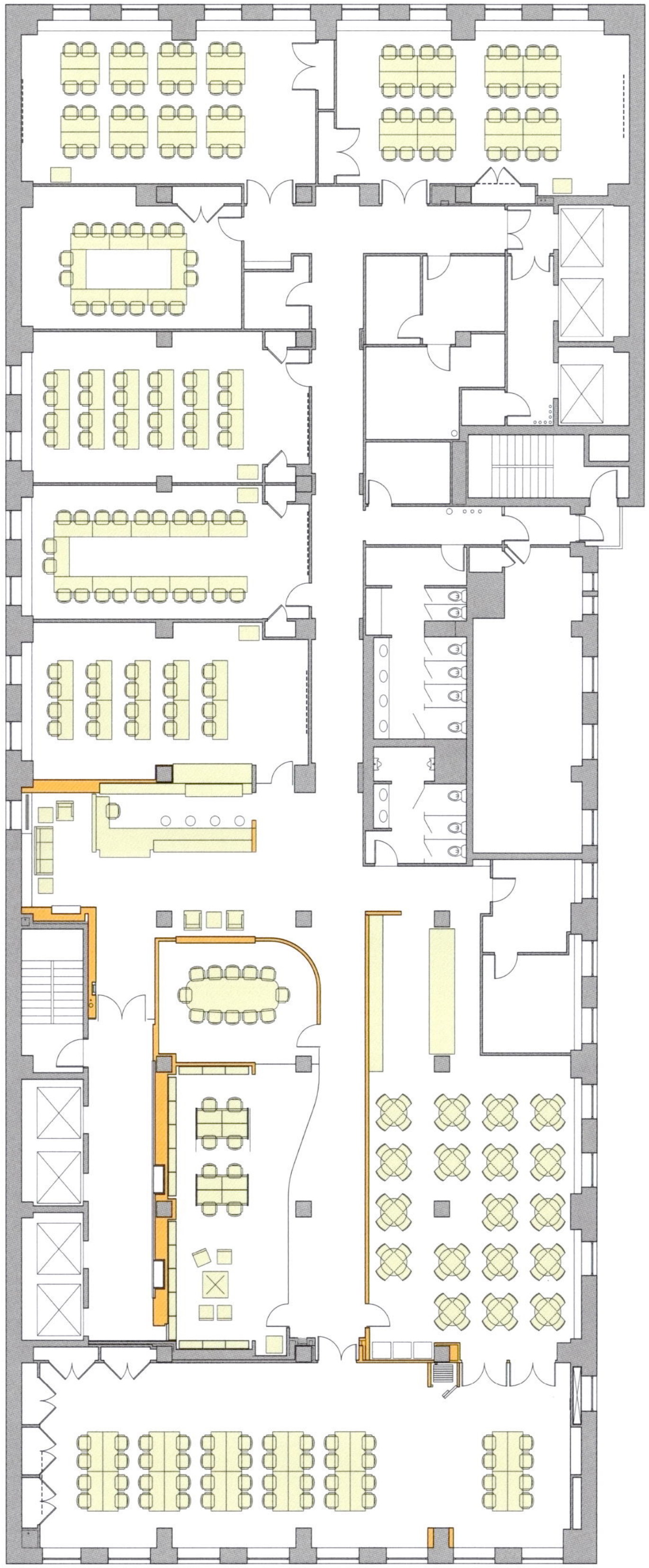

Floor plan

SESQUICENTENNIAL

The project is important for its subtle impression. A soft palette of pastel colors accentuates solid wall surfaces of different shapes and dimensions, uniting the granite, corian, and cherry panel walls and cabinet surfaces. The glass provides transparency, connecting these surfaces and materials. Although the natural materials have a strong presence, the painted surfaces mediate between them and take on the responsibility of coalescing the disparate elements.

Lighting in the space is an important "read." As it is a mid-block building, there is very limited natural light on a typical floor such as this, and of course the rooms at the street-facing window walls are programmed for meeting and conference space. With this being the case, there are only two small window pockets related to light wells between buildings that allow some light into the middle of the plan. In this project, the internal circulation spine is brightly lit, attached to the two small pockets of natural light along its path, giving contrast between natural and artificial lighting. Where natural light contributes to the aura of the space, the artificial lighting is of much-reduced intensity. The effect, and impact, on finish surfaces is dramatic.

EXIT

The Inherent Quality of Materials

Architects work with materials and consider their use in both an unmodified and processed state. Materials exist in their "raw," original form, are refined to change their quality through an artisanal/manufacturing process, or new materials are created.

The work of a few artists—sculptors, notably—have shown that a material can be seen as something immediately recognizable but in its interpretation takes on a different quality; for example, a solid becomes a liquid (Noguchi stones). A material is stretched and shaped beyond normal comprehension (Serra steel panels). Architects sometimes defy gravity (Wright).

The Architect shapes a building from the assembly of systems in three dimensions. Most is hidden. It is the outwardly visible and tactile surface that acquires its reading and definition, through light and color and texture, transparency/opacity/translucency. It is interesting that a surface, or skin, can be perceived as something "thick" or "thin," and in many instances this is the safe and normal way to design. However, as history attests, there has always been a struggle with these perceptions, and architects who think about the subject strive to interpret things on another level. It is the difference between decoration and architecture.

When one thinks of form, it is most often associated with the rendition of a solid with plastic qualities (perhaps with openings). Even a transparent form is a geometry of interwoven skeletal systems of structure and infill. Success in achieving the definition of such form is a "degree zero" of just what it takes to make something recognizable that exists in an otherwise abstract way.

Materials collide when a decision is made to transition from one to another, layer one over another, or physically interlock. It is not a haphazard change but one of relationships bound by a theme. Materials separate when there is a need to use a sum of its parts to make a whole. Materials are continuous when an underlying

Clockwise from top left: The joints separate, the shadow joins; Individual pieces as a whole; The dichotomy of metal and wood—cojoined in detail and reliant on one another; Neutral flat light nonetheless displaying the countless nuances of a surface; Wood, stone, glass, and the lines between

module serves to bind rather than separate. All these decisions and the resulting readings are heightened by light and detail, exemplified in the greatest degree by sun and shadow.

Texture, however shallow or deep it may be—or nonexistant, though that too is a texture—displays the make-up of the material and how it is meant to be perceived. Texture is critical. As light plays across the surface, the material can display other qualities that can be inconceivable in a sample form. Light and shadow transform the material itself.

Harmony under such conditions is when the first, second, one hundredth visit through the space/building is more and more revealing, activating relationships between elements. Perhaps they were contrived as part of the plan and section, but if the conditions are right, it is likely the reality becomes more revealing. This is the importance of consideration of light, color, and texture—material—in the concept.

Age can be thought of as something inherently destructive to a building or space. Climate and the elements typically give an architect cause for concern and always present challenges in assembling and detailing systems and their material make-up. Couple this with the ever-changing technologies in assemblies and the appearance of visible surfaces that must be evaluated for their effect and permanence. A material chosen for its durability is also chosen for its aging process. The tactile quality of a material, whether inherent or manufactured, will transform in appearance and "feel" over time.

With this there are two choices in the manifestation of the design—the surface will disappear into the surroundings, or the surface will continue to stand out. In either case it remains reliant on light to exploit this quality.

Clockwise from top left: Pure texture; Contrasting metal; The connectors allow the materials to be; Raw materials refined; Texture and shadow

Mosaic Pre-K Center

Queens, New York

Transparency in the Park

It is a rare opportunity to design and construct a project within parkland in a city like New York. One of the city's most iconic parks, and the site of two twentieth-century World's Fairs, Flushing Meadows Corona Park encompasses 897 acres bounded by numerous diverse Queens neighborhoods and pierced by highways crisscrossing the borough. Flushing Meadows Corona Park retains much of the layout from the 1939 World's Fair. Its attractions include historical and still popular attractions: the USTA Billie Jean King National Tennis Center, the current venue for the US Open tennis tournament; Citi Field, the home of the New York Mets baseball team; the New York Hall of Science; the Queens Museum; the Queens Theatre in the Park; the Queens Zoo; the Unisphere; and the New York State Pavilion.

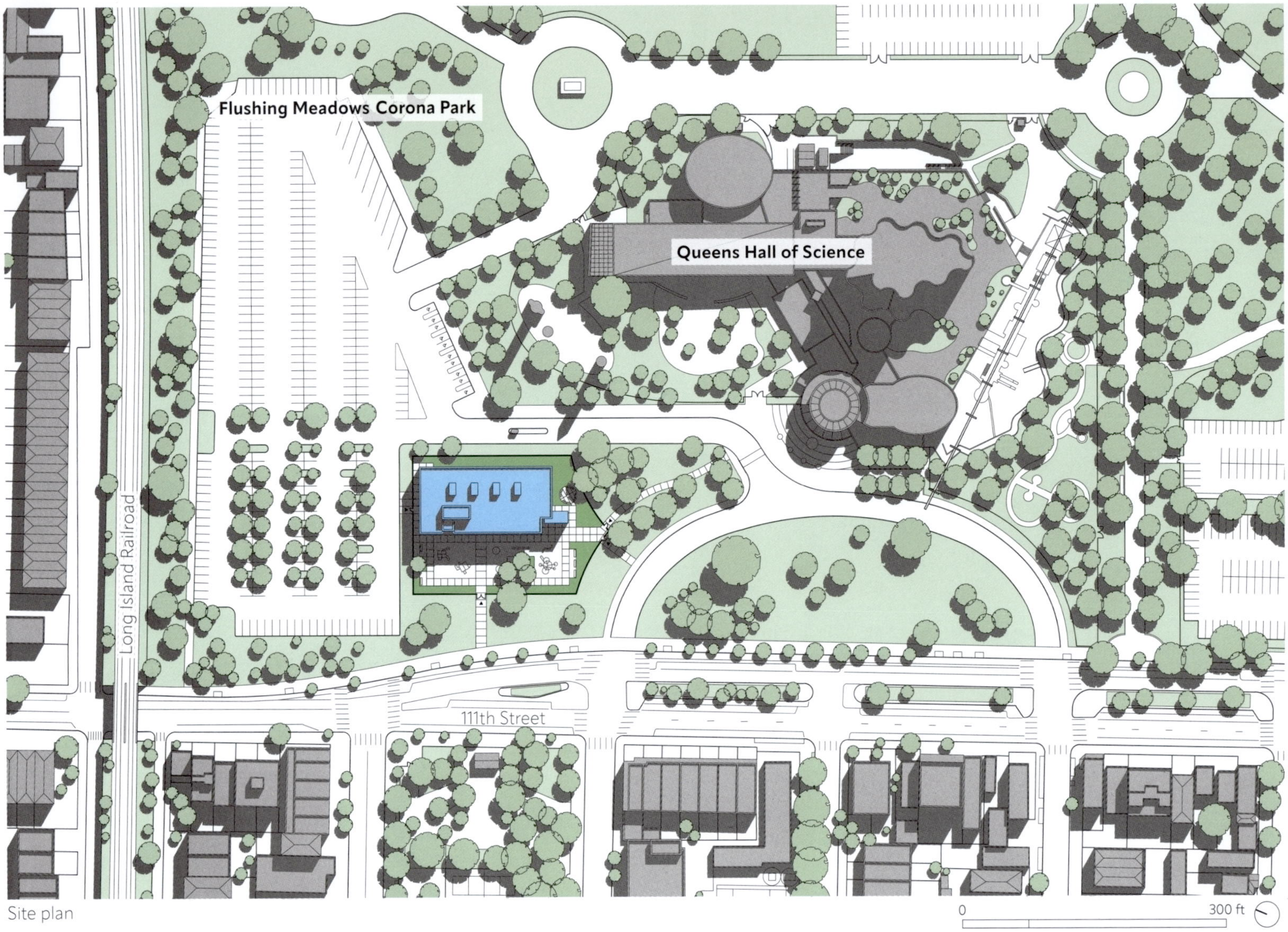

Site plan

This project was initiated as part of the NYC Free Pre-K for All Program for 4-year-olds throughout the City. The Park borders the Corona neighborhood, which has a shortage of school seats for children of all ages, but particularly those of pre-school age. In addition, the NY Hall of Science (HOS) sought a partnership with the Department of Education to create a STEAM curriculum that could be used in a Pre-K program. These conditions fostered zeroing in on a park site near the HOS adjacent to the Corona neighborhood.

Site plan sketch

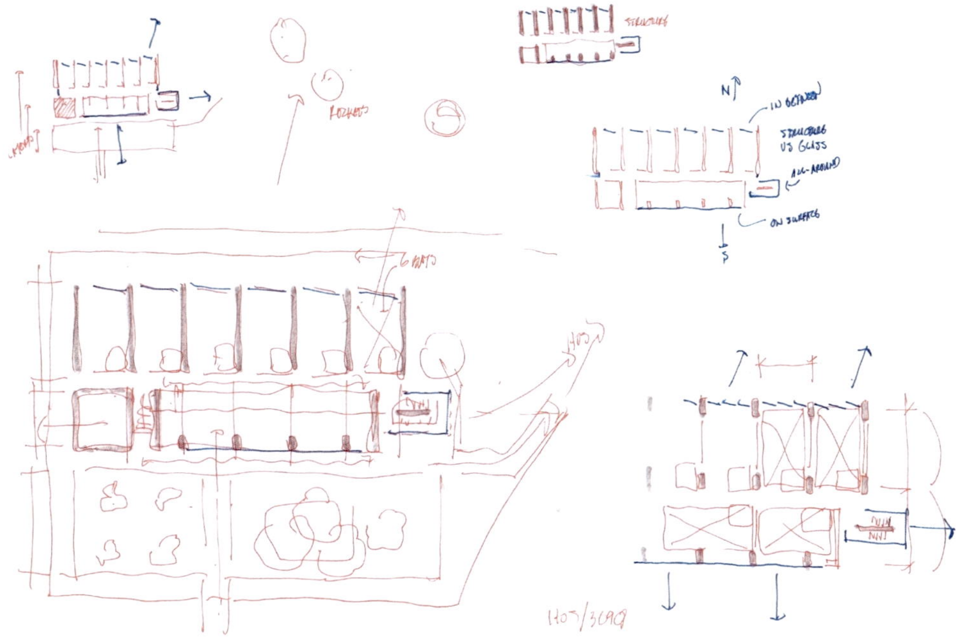
Structural system module

Adding a Pre-K Center within this fabric seems a modest intervention, but engaging with the context to create a distinguished building had to be foremost in the creative process. MDSA had designed a Pre-K Center previously to establish a prototype for such a facility, but the HOS Center was significantly larger and the setting within the park presented issues far outside of the more typical urban block context of the city. The site was set within the park among mature trees and adjacent to the main entry and parking area for the Hall of Science. It was a mix of environments, with a definite "park feel." An axial relationship to a city park across the street, and a direct view of the HOS Rocket Park and the National Tennis Center Stadium set the plan of the building in motion.

Existing structures within Flushing Meadows Corona Park tend to be reserved in their presence within the park. Most are of hard materials and bland colors, with glazed surfaces showing little transparency to the spaces behind (and conversely from inside to the landscape outside). Many are buildings from the World's Fair era that have been adapted to new uses (the National Tennis Center is of course an exception to this). Fundamental to the scheme for the Pre-K Center was to feel the presence of the park and its greenery both from inside the building looking out, and in the immediate site development around the building—play areas, sitting areas and landscaped areas—as it relates to the natural park setting beyond.

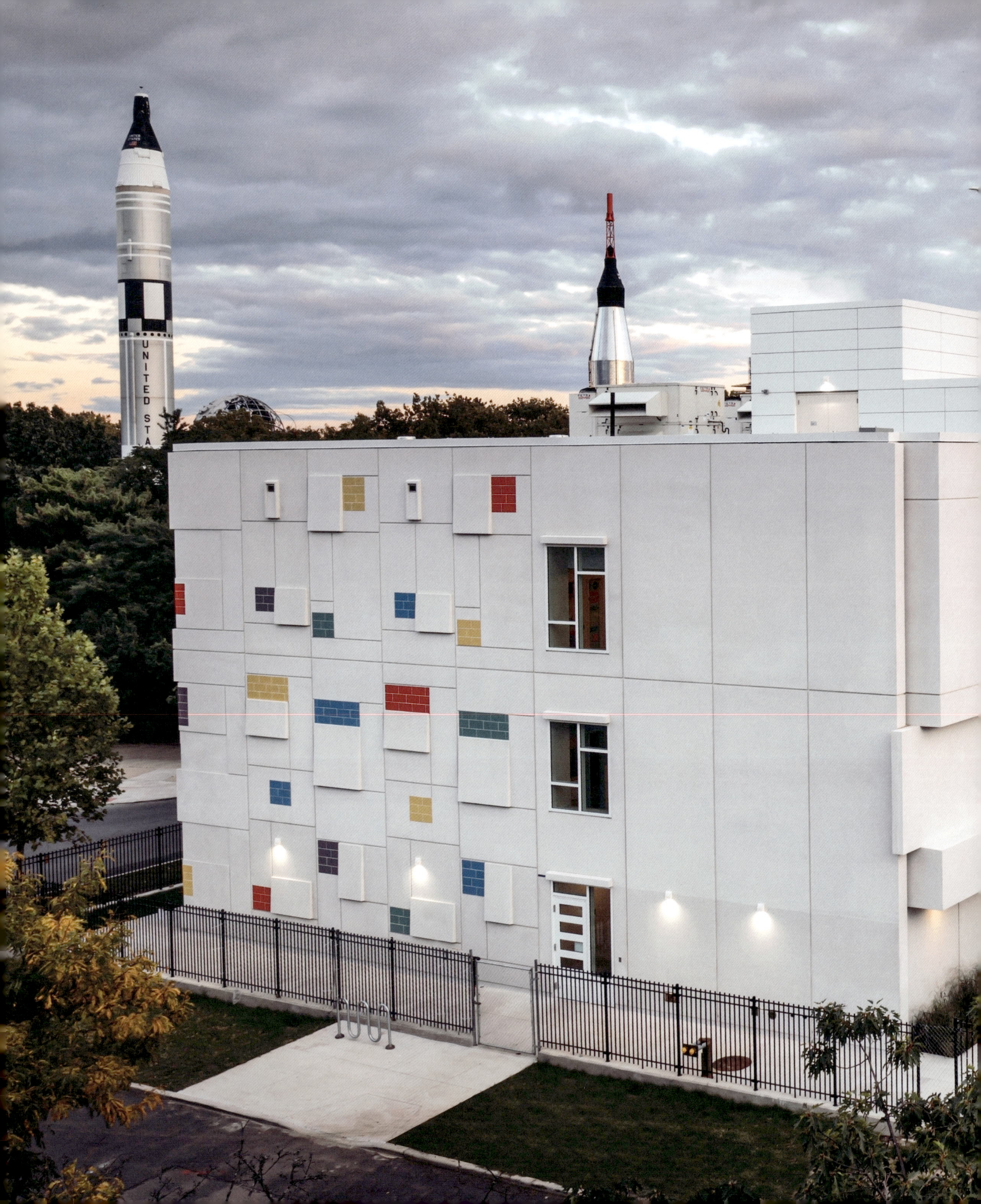
UNITED

TERRACE ON THE PARK

The main element in this relationship is the large, glass-enclosed stair tower, fully transparent and connecting inside to outside. Moving through the stair puts you in the natural landscape, from the lawn areas at ground level and rising through the tree canopy to an elevation giving view to the Hall of Science and its iconic Rocket Park. The stair itself is rotated from the modular 6-bay plan of the school to give a nod to the Hall of Science building. From the stair at ground level is a path leading to the Hall of Science.

The opposite is the case for the other end of the building. Rendered as a solid, this side of the building has less context to respond to—only a large expanse of green space before hitting the park boundary where commuter railroad tracks pass. However, each end of the building shares a deliberate compositional aspect that modulates throughout the rest of the school. A modular grid of white precast panels, broken down into ever smaller grids that derive from other surfaces around the building, including the composition of typical window bay mullions at classrooms. Embedded within this grid system are colorful terra-cotta tiles, seemingly random in pattern, as well as colored glass panels mixed into the mullion grid. The classroom window module at the rear of the school, slightly angled towards the Rocket Park, have a pattern of colored terra-cotta tile surrounds at the window insets. The school became affectionately named "The Mosaic School" because of the patterns of color used throughout the building.

Between the two ends sit 17 classroom modules (for 306 students), the front side comprised of a transparent glass curtain wall, the rear a series of framed openings with large glass window surfaces. The front façade is dramatically affected by the sun over the course of a day and includes many pockets of color originated from within the building that render themselves on the exterior in different ways from day to night. The rear windows are lined with color through indentations of the surrounds and rotated slightly to orient views to the Hall of Science and its Rocket Park.

The building's precast concrete and metal surfaces are white. When thinking about how the building would present itself within such a context, the issue of contrasts became apparent. The green park setting contrasts with the surrounding neighborhood buildings (typically masonry masses), the green park juxtaposed with the blue sky. For this Pre-K white was chosen as a contrast with the surrounding green, embedded within it as a singular object. The elements of color serve to mimic the accents provided by the changing colors of the trees and flowering plants over the change of seasons, bounded by the simple modular volume.

The building is very much a meticulous composition of the exterior skin, orchestrated solids and voids, and colors and textures of materials. The skin, through its transparency and opacity, acts to invite, orient, and control views from outside-in and inside-out. Its presence in the park setting allowed for this unique opportunity to build a relationship between being in the building looking out, and in the park looking in.

Light and Shadow and the Responsibility of the Joint

The juxtaposition of materials is never an overlapping condition. Materials—their textures/colors—do not "blend" together. Their composition is distinguished by their "separation," in the horizontal, vertical, and planar. Light determines how they relate and interact. Viewpoints, be they straight-on or oblique, show continuity or obfuscate relationships, overriding common understandings between elements.

The joint heightens the awareness of the connection between the two materials, at times exploiting the break between them, while other times serving to interconnect like materials seamlessly. The joint can also be its own material with dimension, reinforcing a theme based on modules, proportions, and regulating lines, or incorporating other systems. The mullions of a curtain wall are exemplary of this type of joint.

What is a joint elsewhere can transform to a detail following the regulating lines and order across a façade or interior surface. In such a case we are not speaking of a separation or distinction between materials, but an articulation within the material itself that follows other organizing lines or modules established across the face, be it the façade at the exterior or the surface at the interior. Typically, these are more powerful and understood organizers on a vertical surface as a viewpoint from the observer. The intensely oblique view of the horizontal does not make these relationships as readily apparent.

Clockwise from top left: Mosaic Pre-K Center; Richard Rodgers School PS96X Addition; Mosaic Pre-K Center; Pre-K Center K613

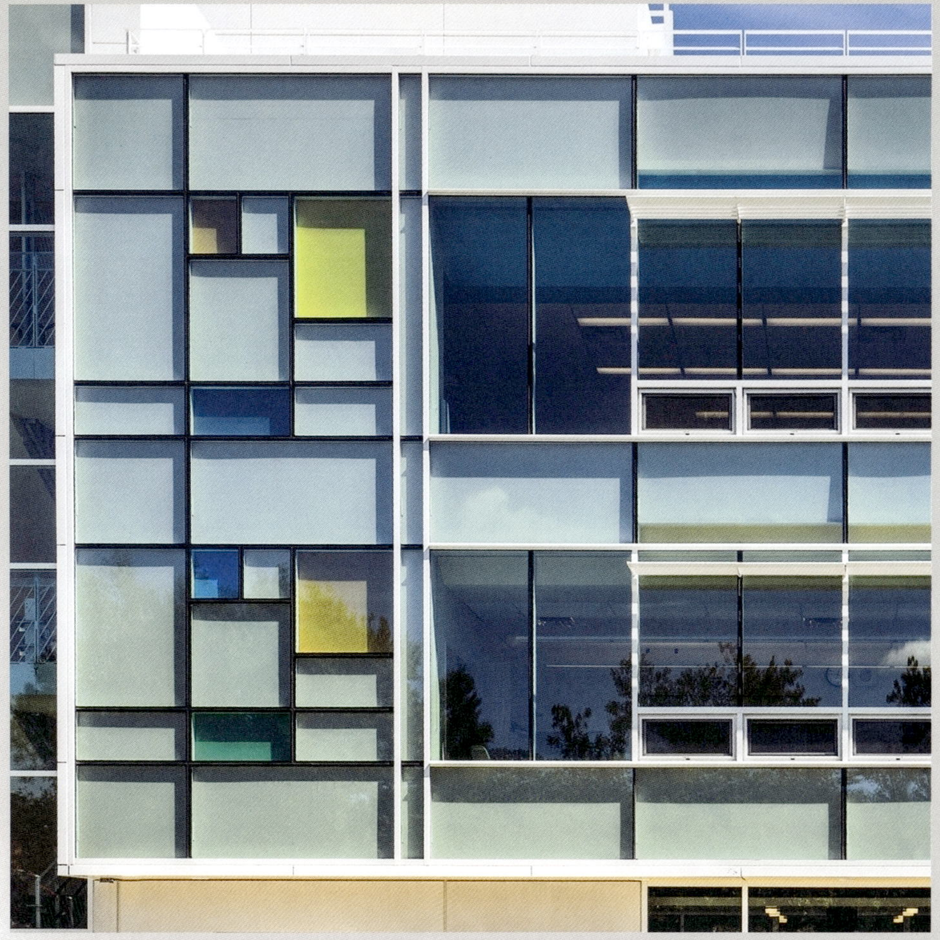

The planar relationship of a surface presents another type of joint, with the addition of depth creating the possibility of an exaggeration of light and shadow. The same separation exists between surfaces, with the anticipation that under timely conditions of sunlight, light and shadow will make its own type of materiality. This type of moment can reveal the honesty with which the tactile surface exists through its make-up; in other words, the stacking of components needed to "build up" and support what is seen at the surface, be it thick or thin.

The composition of the entire material palette can create a flush condition, both in plan, section, and the intersection between the two as they establish the third dimension. There is no difference between horizontal and vertical. Deliberately the two surfaces fold and unfold across a relatively flat surface, one that highlights the tactile/textural qualities of the composed materials. A project inevitably confronts these situations, and conscious decisions can create a harmony of horizontal and vertical, or a deliberate conflict. The joint determines the reading.

The shadow created by the joint gives proportion to a surface and can isolate materials. Commonly the separation is the result of the given size and thickness of products and the patterns created in layout during design. Interestingly these considerations are derived from a purely two-dimensional—elevation or plan—view. The most profound thing that can happen is that the play of light and shadow takes on its own materiality, constantly changing across the surface in intensity, color, and depth.

Clockwise from top left: NYCHA Superstorm Sandy Resiliency & Renewal Program at LaGuardia Houses; NYCHA: Child Care and Community Center at Redfern Houses Complex; Morning Sky House–detail of shadows and textures; Stone and weathered steel; Contrast of bluestone, wallboard and wood flooring

Pre-K Center K613

Brooklyn, New York

Shadow Play

Looking at the figure/ground of the Brooklyn, New York neighborhood where this Pre-K Center is sited, the project disappears into the fabric. It is the roughly textured site area that presented the problem of how to design a building that mediates between being recognizable as a school while blending with the typical small-scale urban area filled with residential blocks. The uniqueness of the site is that the school is mid-block, tucked into the surrounding fabric of brick masonry structures.

The ability to maximize natural light into the spaces, particularly the classrooms, was of major concern. The street façade faces south but the five-story buildings opposite the narrow street blocked sunlight especially in the winter months. The school is set back from the street to give as much opportunity for sunlight as possible, which created a front yard for entry, sitting and play, and mixed well with other setback conditions along the street. Shade control on the façade gives a play of light and shadow within the building when the sun is high in the sky in the summer.

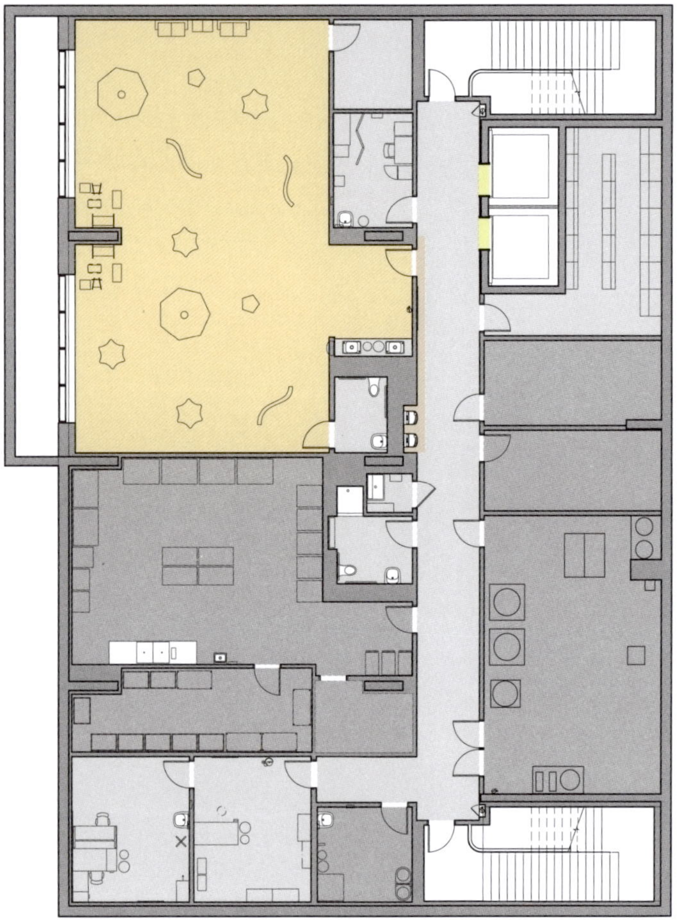

Cellar floor plan

First-floor plan

The plan of the school follows a simple repetitive structural module established by the organization of a basic classroom. The typical classroom, while open and flexible for a variety of arrangements, itself provides an inherent order, established by the rhythm of the window module, door/entry, storage, and toilet elements. The interiors are designed using a variety of materials that tie together corridor and classroom spaces with a soft yet vibrant color palette, playing off the modular system in the detailing of floor finishes, ceilings, and soffits. The school provides 14 classrooms for 252 students and includes a clerestory-lit multipurpose room at the cellar level.

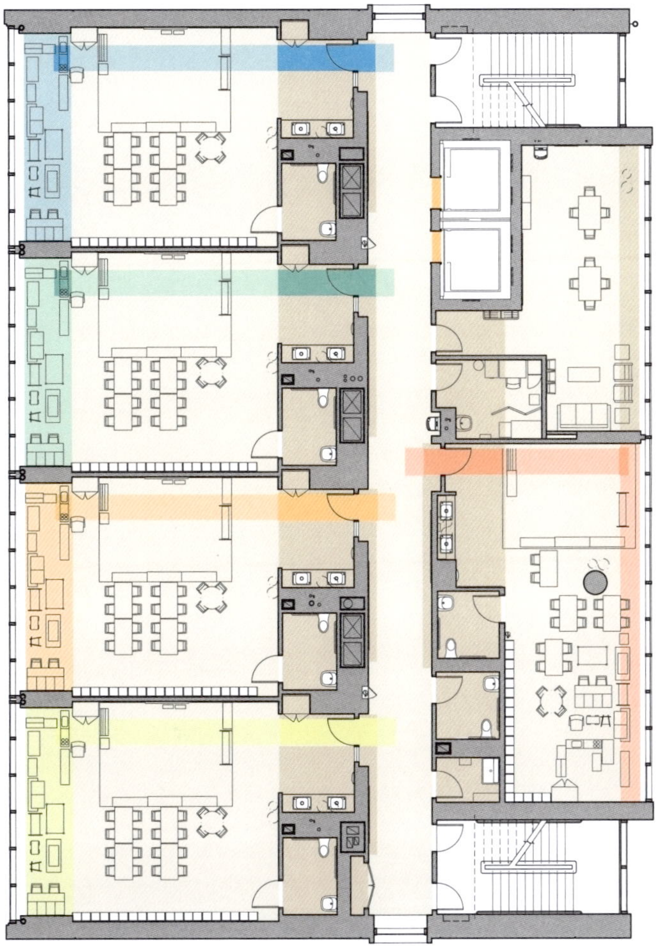
Second-floor plan

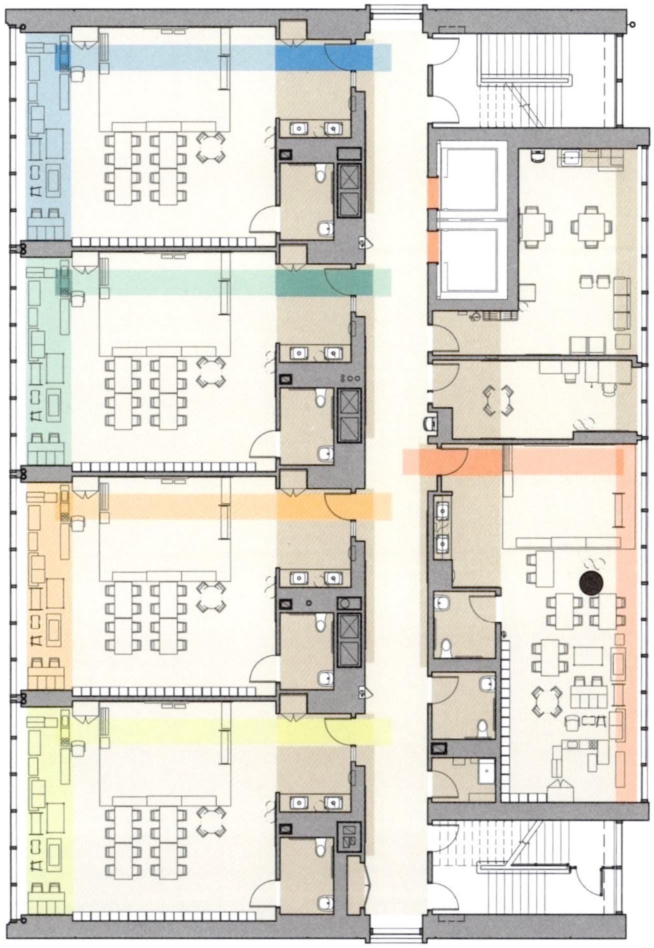
Third-floor plan

Site plan

The school is a very different typology from the rest of the surrounding neighborhood. The prescribed program for the school allowed for the massing to infill the block in a good way. The identity of the building comes from the large glass curtain wall framed by a dark red, metal panel system. End walls are precast concrete mimicking typical solid masonry lot line walls. The blending of the building with surroundings comes from the façade articulation as a system of modular components, in both the horizontal and vertical dimension, that takes a cue from façade elements of adjacent buildings.

NOTICE
NOTICE

The building set a precedent for many schools to follow by using a concrete structure with highly efficient precast concrete panels, curtain wall, and a metal panel rainscreen envelope. Reducing the number of materials/system components and standardizing the attachment of building envelope elements to the concrete frame yielded efficiencies in construction duration and off-site fabrication of systems. This simplification of constructability serves tight urban sites well.

NYCHA Superstorm Sandy Resiliency
& Renewal Program at LaGuardia Houses

Manhattan, New York

A Box in the Park

LaGuardia Houses, located on the Lower East Side of Manhattan, New York City, consists of ten 16-story buildings on an 11-acre site constructed in 1957 and 1965. There are 1,093 apartments on-site with dedicated residences for the elderly. The housing project is typical of the "towers in a park" typology. While the apartment buildings are rather modest mid-rise, brick masonry structures, the park-like setting has extensive lawn areas, playgrounds, and large mature trees. The trees form a near-continuous canopy throughout the site. It can be a quiet island enclave within the surrounding urban fabric. One of the very unique features of the site is a series of formed-concrete, life-size animal sculptures finished with colorful glazed ceramic tiles, located in grassy areas throughout the site. The sculptures were commissioned as part of an art program.

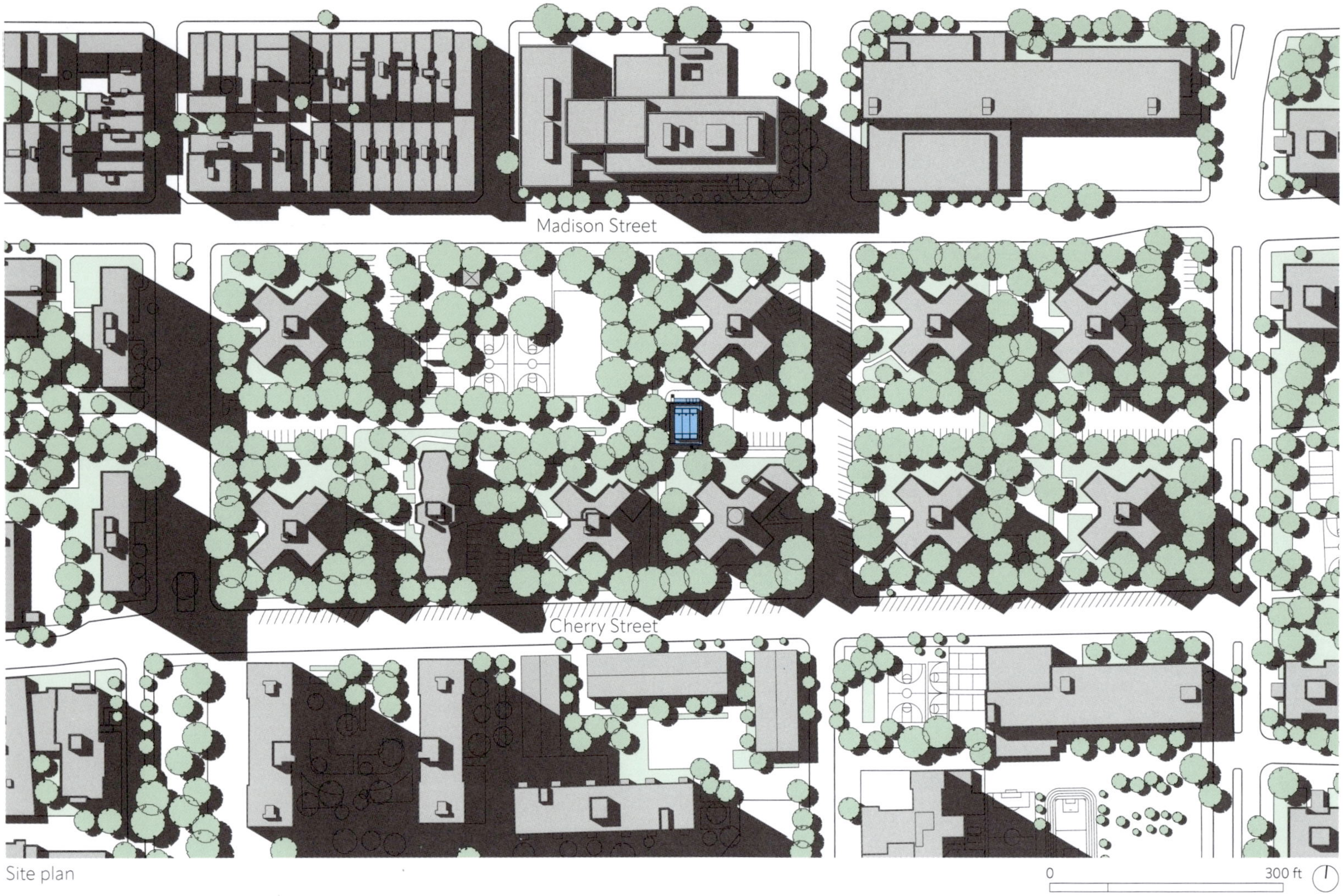

Site plan

Flooding occurred on portions of the site as a result of Superstorm Sandy in 2012, and MDSA completed a project to provide flood mitigation for the affected buildings. Permanent dry floodproofing gates and walls protect existing building services. The jewel of the project, however, is the standalone Electric Service Building, containing emergency generators and incoming site electric service elevated to prevent damage from future flood events.

GENERAC

The structure is not accessible to the public. It stands as its own object, an element formed and articulated solely in response to what it contains. It is watched over by one of the sculptures, a camel. It is a bold, blue color in reference to the other colorful sculptures, meant to share this common theme with the other elements on the site, contrasting with the verdant greenery. The element floats above the ground plane enclosed also with gray fiber-cement concrete panels and metal screens, articulated in such a way as to reference and anchor the building to the adjacent walkways.

Though surrounded by the residential towers, the building is rarely seen from above due to the tree canopy around it. Moving through the site, perspectives of the volume vary dramatically, at times appearing fragmented due to the articulation of the enclosure, with the blue wrapping around and interlocking with the gray. Only a close-up view shows how the building makes itself whole as a composition.

NYCHA: Child Care and Community Center at Redfern Houses Complex

Manhattan, New York

Rising Above

The Redfern Houses complex is a nine-building mid-rise residential development with 604 apartments. Constructed for the New York City Housing Authority (NYCHA) in 1959, the complex is located on an 18.78-acre site in Far Rockaway, Queens. Despite living in a city with 520 miles of coastline, when Superstorm Sandy devastated New York City in October 2012, residents had never grappled with storm surge at that scale. As a result of damage from Superstorm Sandy, NYCHA R&R (Recovery and Resiliency Department) worked with MDSA to design several program elements at the site as part of a comprehensive project to "harden" and protect the site from future storm events. Several structures were built, all elevated above the FEMA-established Design Flood Elevation (DFE) to prevent future damage and loss from a flood or hurricane.

Site plan

0 300 ft

The project comprises a sitewide restoration including improvements and flood proofing of existing residential buildings and new resiliency building additions. The existing residential buildings incorporate wet and dry flood proofing via passive and deployable systems. The new resiliency building additions house relocated major building system components in an elevated structure protected from future flooding.

Second-floor plan

First-floor plan

A new two-story 11,000-square-foot Child Care and Community Center serves residents living in the seven-story residential buildings within the Redfern complex. The program features a childcare center at the entry level with three classrooms for 60 children, a kitchen and administrative spaces on the first floor. On the second floor, the community emergency center contains meeting rooms and a public assembly space with a foldable partition that can accommodate large or smaller gatherings. The center also includes a warming pantry. A large glass curtain wall provides abundant daylight into the interior spaces. The building is sited next to an existing courtyard, which includes a new playground for the childcare center and green spaces for the residents.

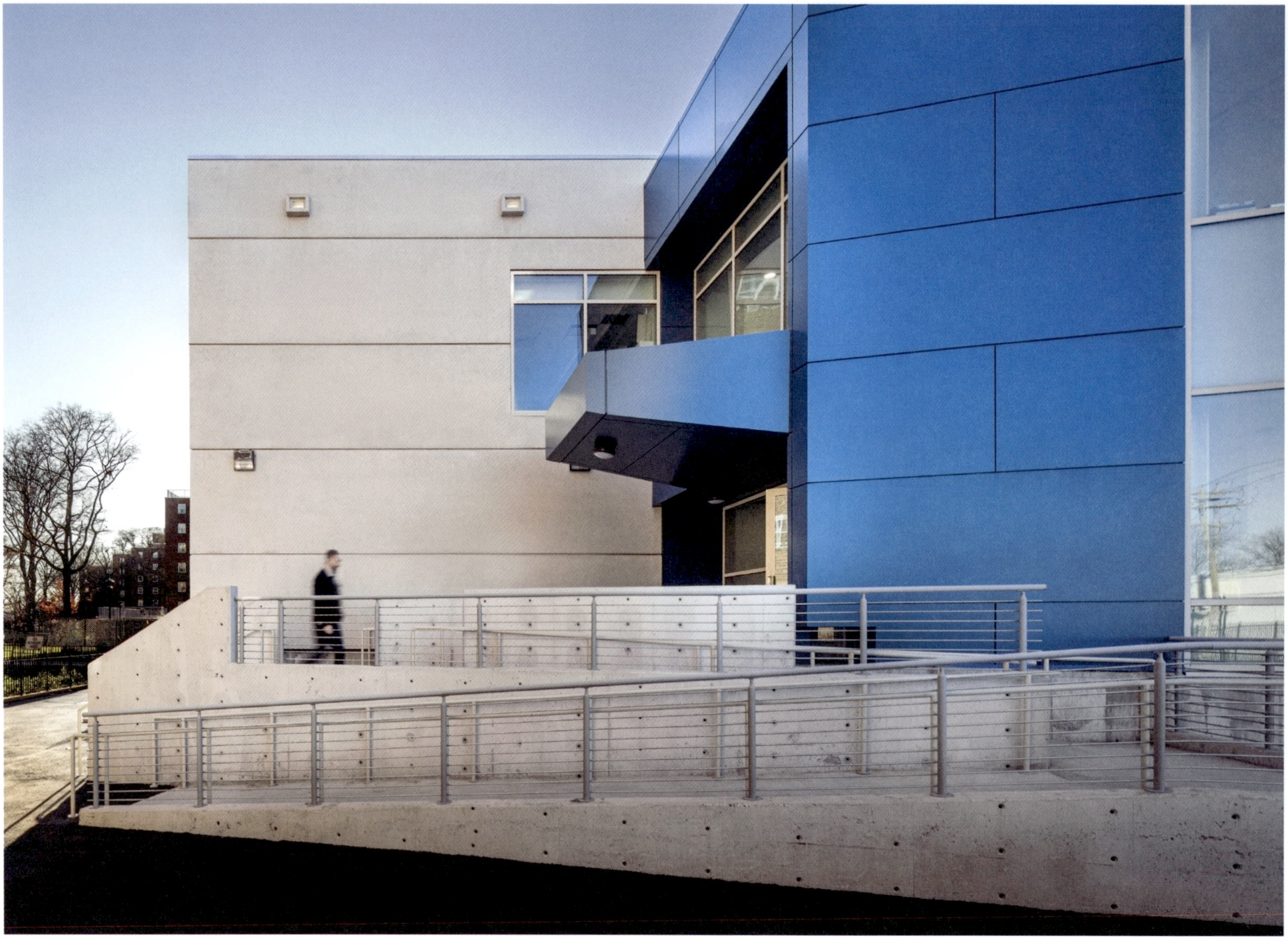

MDSA worked closely with NYCHA R&R and various project stakeholders, city agency representatives and resident groups. The collaborative process played a significant role in shaping the program and scope of the project. The facilities replaced those at the complex that were heavily damaged during Superstorm Sandy in 2012.

At the exterior the Center features a distinctive façade with large glass surfaces (hurricane resistant) and light-toned precast concrete panels giving the building an identifiable presence, while blue metal panels surrounding the entrance and other areas are compatible with the character of the surrounding brick residential towers.

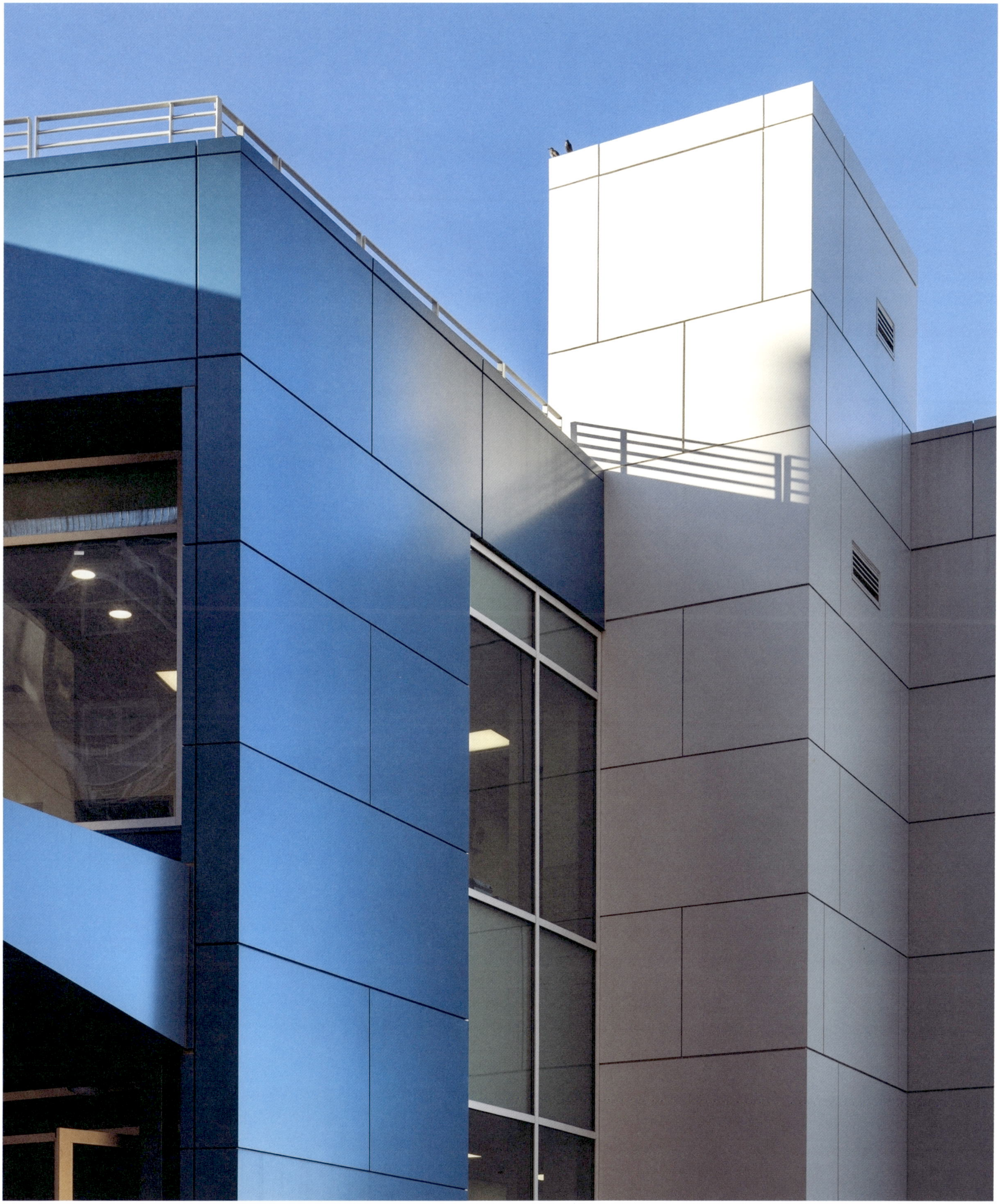

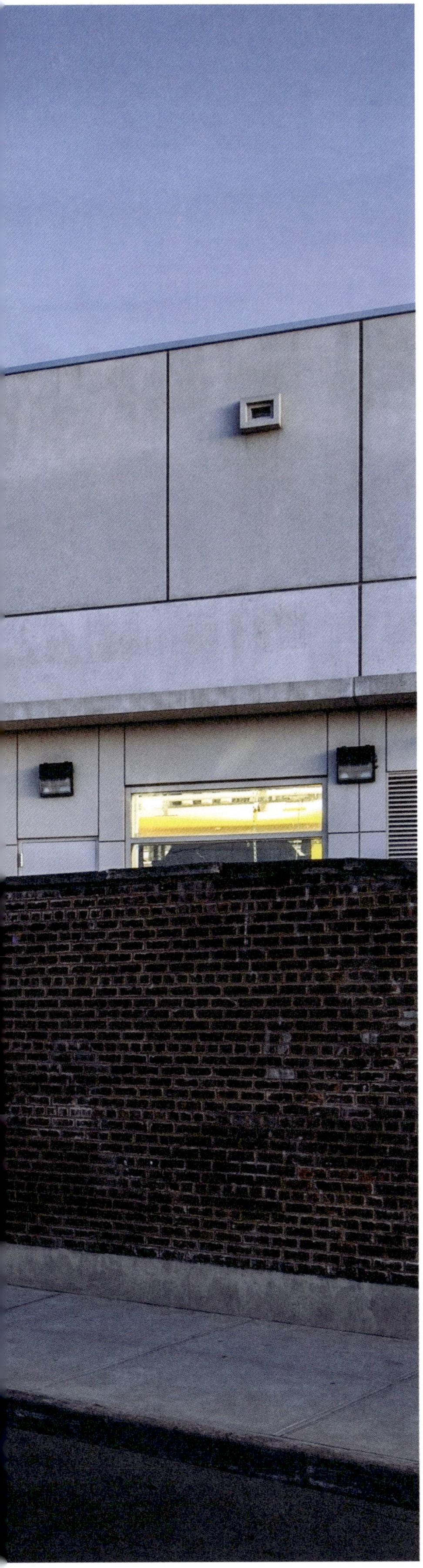

The boiler plant was replaced within a new elevated structure, uniquely situated atop the original coal bunker, which was already above the elevation dictated by the FEMA-established DFE. The boiler plant was a much-needed replacement and energy efficient upgrade to the existing boilers, which (being below grade) were completely flooded. The building enclosure is a high-performance insulated concrete precast panel system.

New electric service buildings were also constructed, also elevated above the FEMA-established DFE to prevent future power loss from a flood event. These structures contain the main electric service for each residential tower and house gas-driven stand-by generators to provide full power capacity for the entire residential complex. These structures, of which there are five, are "sculpted elements" of precast concrete and blue metal panels strategically placed throughout the site, blended with the landscape. The Redfern complex is covered with green vegetation, grass, and large deciduous trees.

The presence of the Community and Child Care Center building, and its related outdoor spaces, has served to revitalize the housing complex. It is an attractive and dynamic structure, unique yet compatible to the rest of the buildings and site. Its visibility from within the complex and related sitting areas and playgrounds make it a focal point for the residents and source of pride—its goal being to make a much-needed program enhancement and upgrade to the 60-plus-year-old complex—for current and future residents.

Origins of a Design Philosophy

The Architect designs, builds, and moves on to the next project. How often does he reflect on the work, over time, the choices made in forming spaces, informing the plan and section? How thoughtful or imaginative was the use of materials—textures, color—as they play with light over the course of a day, the seasons, the years?

How does the symphony of solids and voids, transparency and opacity, define the program and movement through the space? The six surfaces defined by the elements reinforce an idea as you move through the building and/or site, first visually then physically. The "structure," however it is conceived, provides the framework to establish the order of things, and it is the symphony of all the other elements and surfaces that manifest this order as an occupiable physical space.

The composition of elements is described as lines on a plan or section. A space is "measured" in this way, in relationship to both what is expected, and what is to-be-expected. If the Architect is thoughtful and imaginative, these same drawings allude to the unexpected (abstraction), but are nonetheless recognizable. The concept of abstraction pushes architecture forward. Architecture is unique in the arts in that it is grounded in human habitation and occupancy, but it is most interesting when approaching abstraction. That is, the degree at which the most fundamental (minimal) definition of a space/enclosure is understood but extends beyond this established mark.

Opposite: Plan studies for a residence

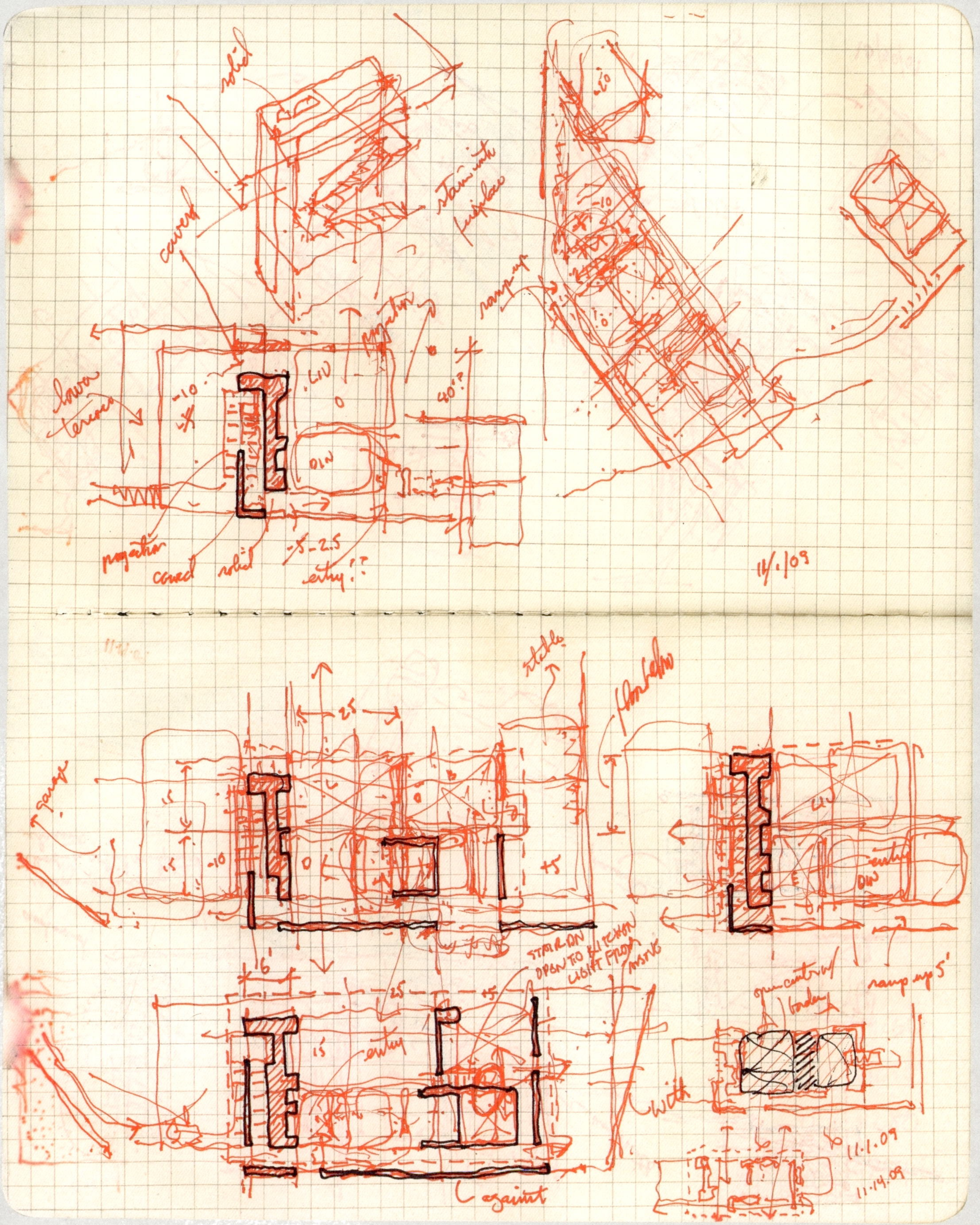
solid
covered
ramp up
projection
lower terrace
LIV
DIN
projection
covered solid
entry!?
11.1.09
garage
25
stable
STAIR ON
OPEN TO KITCHEN
LIGHT FROM
ABOVE
entry
against
with
ramp up 5'
11.1.09
11.14.09

How does the project read—its context, presence, visibility, invisibility? The project is conceived in totality, sometimes building up from numerous pieces into a composition, while other times it is a reduction of a grand idea, breaking into small pieces. Its development, however, should contain a germane idea—measurement, proportion, scale, modularity—that permeates each and every element as it manifests into built form. The user can reliably relate to these organizational principles throughout his/her presence as an occupant, every time. At its most profound, new revelations occur from time to time. This reflects the degree of study exhibited by the design, and gives the observer points of reflection and an understanding of relationships between spaces and program.

Opposite: Site Plan Sketch for Sho Fu Den Retreat

MAGNETIC NORTH
SEPTEMBER, 2004
15.33 ACRES
convert to hall
service
japanese garden
garden court
entry
courtyard gardens
terrace
parking?
SCHEME
1 o the natural landscape garden
2 o the courtyard gardens
3 o the walks / connections / paths
4 o the structures around the courts SECTION!
CERTIFIED TO
SHO FU DEN, LLC
woods

Universal Physical Education Gyms

Brooklyn, Queens, and the Bronx, New York

Changing Face

New York City Public Schools initiated the Universal Physical Education Program, targeting existing elementary schools that lack an indoor gymnasium. The site for the projects uses a portion of the school play yard to construct stand-alone multipurpose gym buildings, enabling students to have large physical activity space year-round under all weather conditions.

The existing schools were typically constructed in the early 1900s, some historically significant, registered with the New York State Historical Preservation Office. As such, the prototype design and its variations are contextual with the original masonry buildings with appropriate detailing at the base, cornices, and window surrounds.

The challenge in creating a prototype is to find pervasive themes in the existing building envelopes to develop a standard façade system that can permit adjustments in the design to allow for compatibility from site to site. To provide an adaptable system, MDSA utilized structural insulated precast concrete panels that permit modulation and modification of the exterior surface in its detailing to fit existing contexts. The system is also highly efficient regarding structural integration, energy efficiency and erection time.

MDSA has a long history stemming from the firm's legacy of innovation in the use of precast concrete and detailing thereof. The predecessor firm's work is cited numerous times in the industry standard PCI Handbook. Due to the plastic nature of concrete, the possibilities are infinite in the articulation of joints, modulation, planar relationships of surfaces, and incorporation of other materials into the concrete itself.

MDSA developed a prototype design to a wide range of urban school sites. The prototype design was then tailored to each of ten school sites throughout the boroughs of Brooklyn, Queens, and the Bronx. Scope of work for each site varied depending on existing site conditions and added amenities desired by the client and user. Playgrounds, turf soccer fields, and landscaping were included in the design of some sites.

Exterior envelope detailing was revised for each project to relate to the color of existing building surfaces as well as the rhythm and detailing of the fenestration. These revisions produced a range of unique buildings, maximizing the efficiency of applying the prototype design to many sites. Design schedules were thus greatly reduced due to MDSA's ability to quickly adapt the prototype to each site.

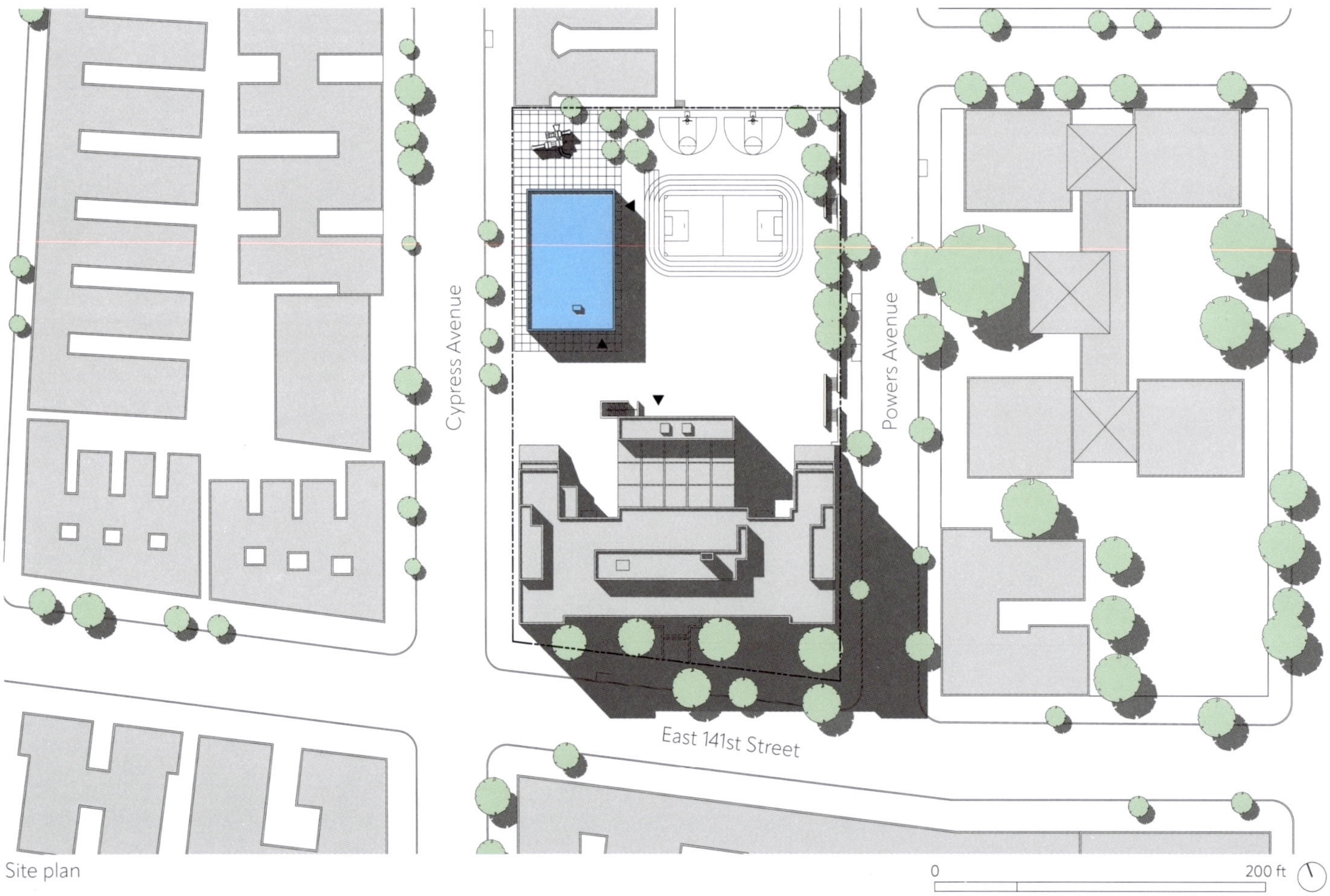

Site plan

5
5

4
5
6
7
8
9
10
EXIT

Site analysis for each site revealed basic prototype modifications that could be implemented to coordinate the prototype design with unique features of each site. Alternate plans were created to allow for opposite-hand entrances to maintain direct connections to the existing school. Alternate foundation and precast base details were developed for sites with varying grades.

The result is a series of gymnasiums neatly integrated into the school sites, each with unique modern detailing, forming a strong relationship with the existing school buildings.

Ocean Bay Apartment (Bayside)
Sandy Resiliency & Renewal Program

Far Rockaways, Queens, New York

Bayside Blue

This project, seemingly not your classic architectural problem, ended up serving to revitalize a very large site gridded with 24 mid-rise residential towers. Controlling the ground plane and defining pockets of space provided a sense of place at the resident/pedestrian scale. The site plan organizes and connects residual space between buildings, linking exterior program with thoughtful connections as they engage the building entries with the surrounding city block-grid. It creates horizontal order within the vertical figure/ground of the towers.

In the aftermath of Superstorm Sandy in 2012, NYCHA embarked on a recovery program by performing extensive building damage assessments and installing temporary electrical switchgear, and temporary mobile boilers to restore the habitability of the residential buildings in the most severely affected developments. The project was called the "Sandy Resiliency & Renewal Program."

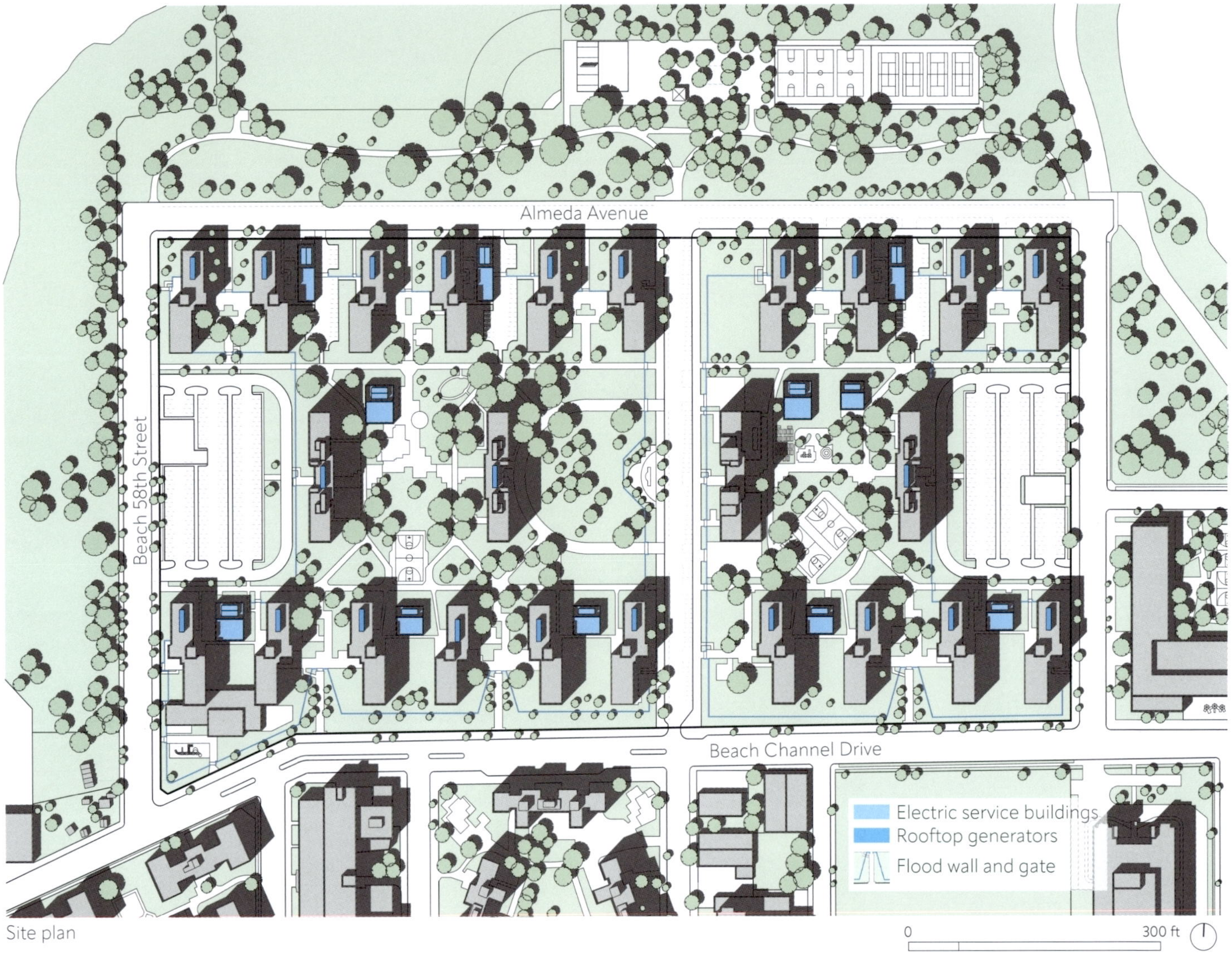

Site plan

MDSA was engaged to provide architectural services and collaborate with its team of site/civil and structural engineering consultants to create permanent solutions to prevent future damage from hurricane or flooding events at the Ocean Bay Apartments (Bayside) housing complex.

The Ocean Bay Apartments (Bayside) complex comprises 24 apartment buildings with 1,395 apartments providing housing for over 6,000 residents located on a relatively flat 32-acre site. The complex consists of 20 seven-story buildings around the perimeter of two city blocks, and four nine-story buildings centrally located within the sites.

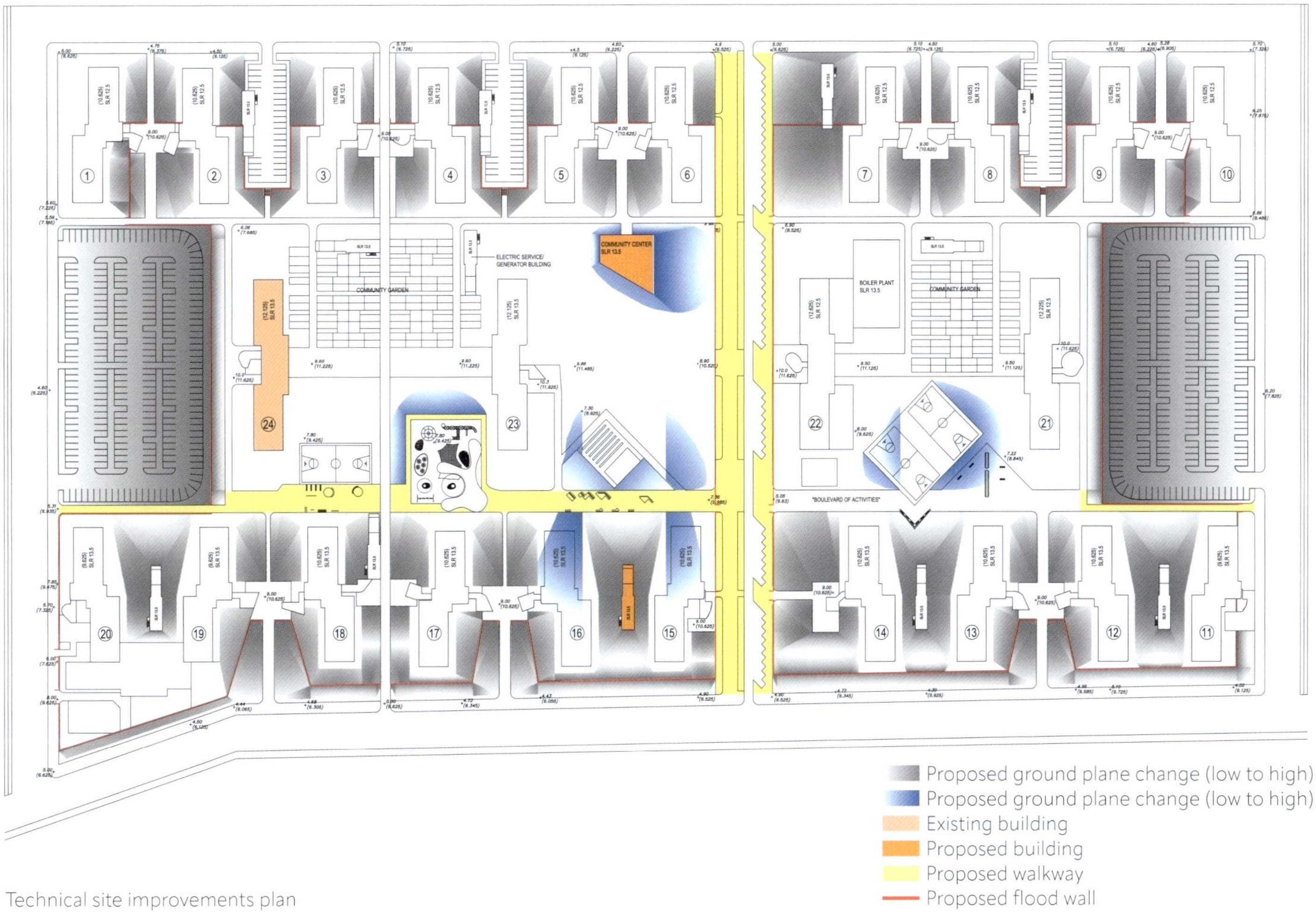

Technical site improvements plan

The program was developed to provide flood protection of the site, following FEMA-established Design Flood Elevation (DFE) prescribed requirements, for primary electric service, residential building envelope (dry and wet floodproofing), and building entries. The project cost exceeded $222 million. The solution involved the following major elements.

A perimeter flood wall, over 5,200 feet in length, encircles the 32-acre site to prevent surface flood waters from entering above grade, and subsurface water seepage below grade. The flood walls are visually hidden through use of sloped berms of the finish grade, and nicely landscaped. Where the building entries face streets, protective flood walls and panels for the building lobbies were added. The flood walls rise above grade creating portals signifying the access points to the towers and main walkways.

Any break in the flood wall is protected with a system of flood panels that automatically rise during flood conditions to prevent water infiltration into the "moated site;" all 32 acres. The series of pedestrian and vehicular passive flood panels are integrated with the flood walls and seal the openings with gasketed panels.

424 BEACH 58TH STREET

A series of single-story buildings, whose floor elevations are above the FEMA-established DFE, are located throughout the site, containing new building electric service and standby emergency generators that provide full electric capacity for the complex should power be disrupted.

OCEAN BAY

Across a 32-acre low-lying site, not far from the Atlantic Ocean, the existing topography appears completely flat. In fact, conditions varied up to eight feet in elevation. Gradient studies determined an average baseline across numerous sections through the site, and indicated pockets of depressions and rises in grade. The locations were critical to any site planning and the formation and location of accessible pathways throughout the area. The problem was compounded by the bisection of the site by a city street, which had its own existing parameters of elevation and pitch. As water seeks a horizontal elevation, the wall of the protective moat had to match this elevation and be hidden from view through use of berms and tilting of the ground plane. Across such an expanse many of these features go unnoticed visually. Where prominent, the concrete surfaces are clad in varied bluestone planks and panels, mortar-set in the horizontal and vertical applications to render a monolithic enduring finish.

One of the issues with creating a ringed enclosure to prevent flooding of the site from surface water or seepage from below over a multi-hour event, is the wall also acts as a bathtub, containing any water that lands within the site area, as well as from building roofs (since drainage water cannot be released into a system that is pushing water in the opposite direction). The solution expands the existing depression areas within the site to create large water detention ponds, temporarily retaining the internal site overflow until conditions allow for its release from the site area. Commonly called swales, these large areas are defined by natural landscaping, in some instances becoming community gardens for the residents.

In summary, the problem the project presented from a technical site-engineering perspective allowed for a solution that enlivened the ground plane occupied by the surrounding towers with subtle but recognizable place-making with a variety of connections. Both landscaping and activity spaces contribute to the newly defined site.

Early Childhood Education and the Influence of Color

Probably no other project type influenced the work of the firm regarding the use of color than early childhood facilities. This includes work in the 3-K, Pre-K, and elementary school areas. The color palettes, carefully derived from the intimately scaled spaces and their interaction with both natural and artificial light, extend to how the firm approaches higher education, public, and private work.

Typically, the early childhood education projects found themselves located within a variety of situations—new construction, major renovation, tenant fit-out within existing buildings—with each presenting differing conditions of how light was introduced into the program areas. In these situations, materials were basic, so the way that color was introduced under both natural and artificial lighting conditions required careful study. Direct and indirect light from skylights, glaring light from windows, diffuse light from windows, and artificially lit interior spaces were among the conditions under which colors were incorporated.

While an overall color scheme—commonly "wayfinding" or "feature" color systems—may be considered appropriate, MDSA's work stems more from relationships to given lighting conditions, as noted above, and to provide linkage between spaces, rather than segregate areas from one another. The connection between a classroom/meeting room and corridor is an example. It is about allowing, through the use of color, lines to be crossed and spaces penetrated to make connections, visually moving the eye through a building, which in turn offers encouragement of physically moving as well.

Clockwise from top left: Pre-K Center K613; Detail of staircase at The Sixth Avenue Elementary School PS340M; Jamaica Center Pre-K playroom; The Sixth Avenue Elementary School PS340M; The Sixth Avenue Elementary School PS340M

6

EXIT

This is very different from the composition of materials and their joinery. There is little to no texture or tactility to work with, so the idea is made clear solely in the interaction with the surrounds, as a field, pattern or overlapping of horizontal and/or vertical surfaces (floor, wall, ceiling). The interaction with light is not textural, producing shadow, but calling attention to a surface area, be it horizontal or vertical.

The firm's projects use a palette of color as an overall organizer, with the illusion of transparency through overlapping layers of similar color value, or a simple approach to color balance to impact the overall look and feel of a space. Generally, pastel colors, offering high brightness but low saturation, are versatile in this regard. Solids (primary) are reserved for impact or identity, dispersed in small patches that are not meant to dominate. Often, seemingly mundane areas are featured, given a chance to contribute to the overall impression of a space.

Clockwise from top left: The Sixth Avenue Elementary School PS340M; Battery Park Pre-K Center hallway; The Sixth Avenue Elementary School PS340M; Light reflecting onto glass dividers at Jamaica Center Pre-K; Jamaica Center Pre-K detail of skylight; Battery Park Pre-K Center school room

Richard Rodgers School PS96X Addition

Bronx, New York

Respecting the Original

Public schools in dense urban environments such as New York City tend to dominate the neighborhood fabric around them. The sites are half occupied by the building and half by open outdoor play areas, with the building massing overshadowing the surrounding smaller residential and commercial structures. The establishment of schools in this context brought with them a responsibility to be a strong presence, which sometimes includes ornate articulation of façade elements. Over time, as zoning and other regulations change, the surrounding neighborhoods are transformed, leaving the school building as one of the few recognizable anchors of an area. Religious buildings play a similar role in such contexts.

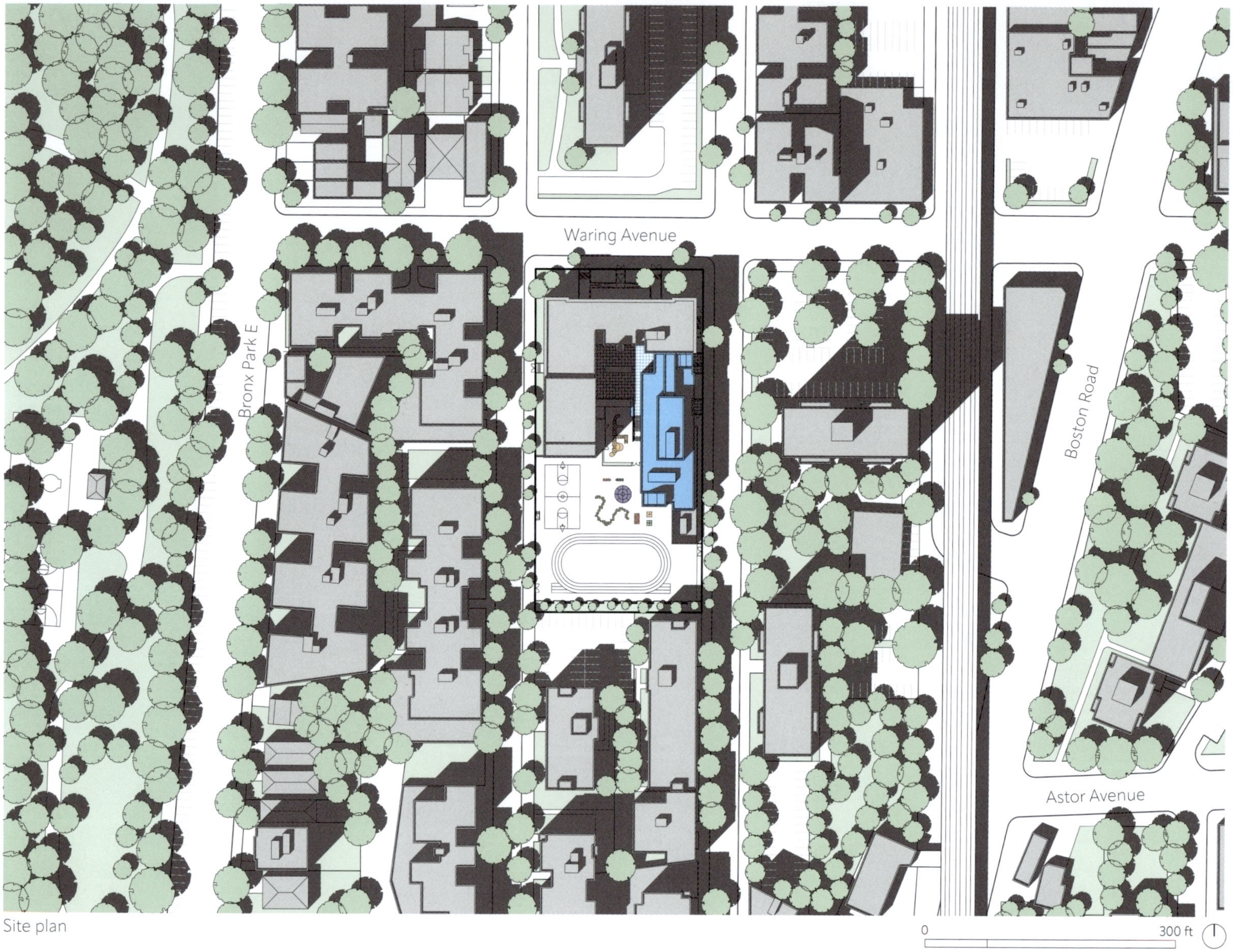

Site plan

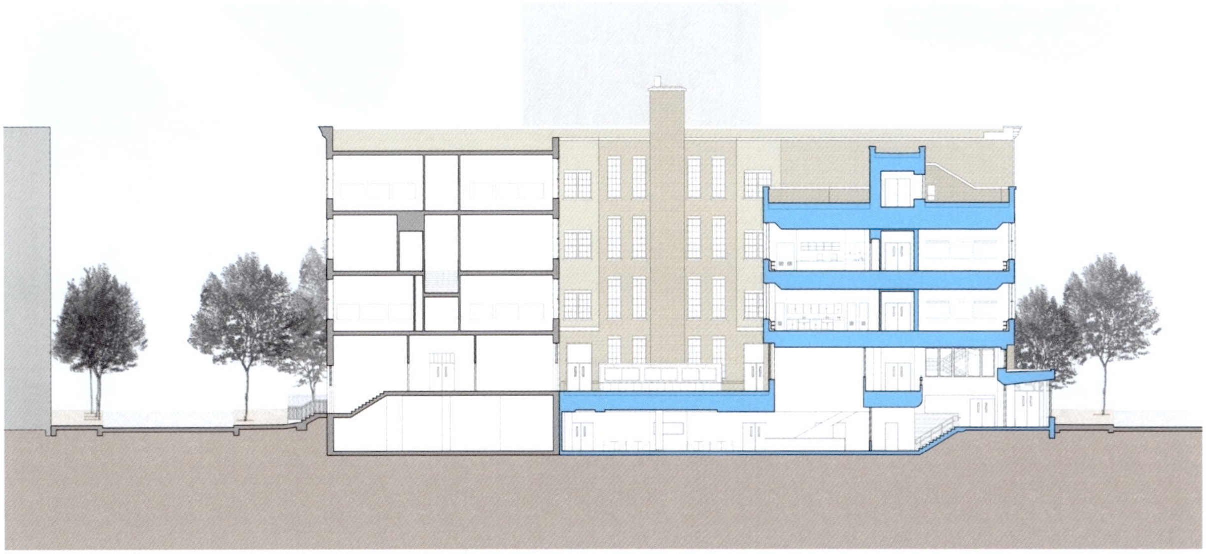

Section

Elevation

The existing public school is a New York State registered historic building constructed in the early 1900s. The new five-story addition (50,000 square feet) to the existing school (66,000 square feet), includes classrooms for Kindergarten through Grade 5 as well as specialized instruction for art and music.

MDSA examined the exemplary massing, materials, fenestration, and detailing of the original building in the conceptual phase, looking to create relationships to the historic structure. While highly detailed with intricate brick and stonework, the building is "flat" on the surface, reliant on small variations in the surface plane and material texture to create interest with shadows. The addition relates to the historic massing, module, and proportions, but breaks from the flatness by breaking down the massing with deep overhangs and a play of opacity and transparency to distinguish the new from the original. Even elements such as window surrounds and copings exaggerate their projection/recess as related to the wall plane to create deep shadows. The solid materials used—brick and cast stone—simply respect the history of the original.

RICHARD RODGERS SCHOOL
EXIT 5
EXIT 5

The site of the building and adjacent yard sloped such that the main level of the original building was elevated one story above the play yard in the rear of the site. The addition exploited this condition by combining a respect for the site section with a floating volume extending from the main building, harmonized through its massing and proportional fenestration. Horizontal regulating lines knit the façades together and window openings matched the existing in size. The large openings allow daylight to penetrate deep into the interiors of the addition.

The addition locates itself as an added leg to the existing 'L-shaped' building, resulting in a 'U-shaped' structure. As a result of the sloping site, the new entry is mid-level relative to the existing floor elevations. This arrangement permitted high ceilings and large glazed surfaces, allowing daylight to penetrate obliquely through the lobby space into the cafeteria below. Centrally located as an infill element at the basement level, the cafeteria serves as a "collector" of the major vertical circulation elements of both the existing building and new addition. The cafeteria faces south and directly accesses the play yard, which allows it to also serve as line-up space, offering three major routes into the main school building. The roof of the cafeteria can be used as a large outdoor terrace for school activities.

Peripheral Vision

A camera can capture an image in infinite ways. Typically, the focus is on the widest range and foreground/background "view," perfectly precise in its impression from edge to edge, as if we see the world under such a condition. But look closely at the colors, texture, and play of light. Focus on a "moment," the detail, and the adjacent context is blurred. Of course, we immediately scan to the next point of focus and the perception shifts, depth is perceived differently, and the visual range (left/right, up/down) takes the eye on an ever-changing journey. It is much the same as looking at the canvas of a master painting.

In the case of a building or landscape, the visual detail, the "moment," gets strength from its surroundings. By visual detail we mean the color, texture, and play of light of the focal point. The immediate adjacency is a blur but still forms a crucial background, in the same terms as color, texture and light, to the overall balance of the composition. It is here that the viewer can recognize the thoughtfulness of the entire project, and devotion to making it a complete work.

The peripheral view can take on a tactile quality. The play of light and shadow can effectively dissolve the areas outside the focal point, while at the same time providing a type of abstract context for the project. It is something perhaps not conceivable in design, but a reinforcer of how well the entirety of the project has been stage-set, the success of the material palette, colors, and textures chosen, and how they lay in relationship to one another.

The cone of vision can be highly focused—centered—knocking out everything around it. There can also be a perceived horizontal, vertical or oblique that is alluded to through the fuzzy lines, colors and textures that move the eye around. These are very deliberate gestures in a well-conceived work, stemming from regulating lines, color arrangements/patterns, and textures. Seemingly disparate relationships can be bound together through these connections.

Clockwise from top left: A single pop of color as the center of attention; Precision of a surface against the blur of the surroundings; Looking through the foreground to the surface beyond; Simultaneity–no hierarchy in a complex layering; Texture exaggerated by sunlight

It is important to consider that such an enlightened view has roots in what is not seen. As the journey is taken with the eye the moments add up in layers. Space can be flattened, compressed. Richness comes in the recognition that a moment has been seen before in some other part of the puzzle, be it a literal repeat but on a different surface and orientation, or simply the fragments of previously established order. In either case, the reference is back to the whole of the project.

What is brought into detail focus—foreground, background, middle-ground—depends on light. Light reflects color and exaggerates texture and casts shadows. This is permitted to happen in a unique moment and is not a continuous event. This is what is important about the need for all the materials, colors, and textures to reinforce an idea. Over time, everything about the project is grounded to the single concept of (in)visibility.

Clockwise from top left: The shadow as material, made by the relationship with everything around it; The intensity of light and shadow on the colors in middle-ground; Depth of field impacted by the glow of light; Rotating orientations of a natural material under a glow of light; Weathering steel panels under a particularly atmospheric condition

Firm History—Precedents to the Work of MDSA

Herbert Beckhard, FAIA, and Frank Richlan, AIA, co-founded the firm, then known as Herbert Beckhard Frank Richlan and Associates (HB+FR), as a successor firm to the office of the late Marcel Breuer, a major figure of twentieth-century architecture and design. Breuer established his original office in New York City in 1946, which he led until his retirement in 1976. Some of his most notable buildings include the Whitney Museum of American Art in New York and the UNESCO Headquarters in Paris. Among many honors, Breuer was awarded the Gold Medal of the American Institute of Architects.

In 1951, Herbert Beckhard began working with Breuer in New York. He became his design collaborator and, in 1964, his partner. During their twenty-eight years of working together, Beckhard and Breuer designed many notable projects such as the H.U.D. Headquarters Building and the Hubert H. Humphrey Building, both in Washington, D.C.; the University of Massachusetts Campus Center in Amherst; the St. Francis de Sales Church in Muskegon, Michigan and the Koerfer House in Ascona, Switzerland. The latter two projects received the prestigious American Institute of Architects National Honor Award. Beckhard was the collaborating partner with Breuer on numerous iconic house designs.

Frank Richlan joined the office of Marcel Breuer in 1968 and became an Associate in 1970. He served as project architect on major projects in the Breuer office, working with Beckhard on many of them. In 1982, following Breuer's retirement and then death, Beckhard and Richlan formed Herbert Beckhard Frank Richlan and Associates (HB+FR). Together, they designed a wide variety of projects that have been recognized with numerous design awards and extensive publication here and abroad. Michael Szerbaty joined the firm in 1985, became an Associate in 1991 and a partner in 2000.

Clockwise from top left: (all designed by HB+FR) Calumet Manufacturing Center; West Brighton Community Center; Prospect Heights Care Center; Franklin Township Technical Center Cornell **Following pages:** Cornell ILR School Entry Plaza

Firm transition occurred in 2003 with the untimely deaths of the two founding partners. The firm has since been under the leadership of Principal Michael Szerbaty, AIA, and since 2014 practices with partner Michael Freedman, AIA, who began his professional career with the firm in 2000 after receiving his degree in Architecture.

The work of HB+FR consistently examined material usage and detailing. Composition and juxtaposition of materials, and technically precise detailing stemming from inventive applications of construction standards were hallmarks of the firm's buildings and interiors. The work continually utilized innovative material textures originating from developments in the manufacturing process (stone and masonry finishing, metal fabrications, casework detailing).

MDSA continues the legacy, reflecting a distinctly contemporary evolution of core modernist principles established by the firm. Influences in the firm's work are recognizable, even as the approach and aesthetics evolve. The clarity and technical precision in the use of materials, and the study in detail of how things are assembled to achieve the outward appearance, permeate the self-critical thought process of the firm, reflective of its predecessors. The use of natural materials, in both raw and refined states (textures), continues as a consideration in how a space is conceived and manifests itself. A fundamental palette of color provides a foundation from which new solutions evolve.

Clockwise from top left: Kwok House, Herbert Beckhard Architect; Detail of railing, Kwok House; Cornell ILR School Phase I; Cornell ILR Catherwood Library roof detail; Cornell ILR Catherwood Library; Cornell ILR School Phase I; Cornell ILR School Phase I (Cornell ILR designed by HB+FR)

Project Credits

The Sixth Avenue Elementary School PS340M (p20–33)
Location: Manhattan, New York
Client: NYC School Construction Authority
Size: 95,000 sq ft
Cost: $42,000,000
Completed: August 2014
Photography: Jon Reis with Dede Hatch / Jon Reis Photography

Morning Sky House, Guest House and Stable (p34–53)
Location: Cottonwood, Arizona
Client: Michael Szerbaty and Janet Twyman
Size: Main House 2,800 sq ft, Guest House/Horse Stable 750 sq ft
Cost: $1,200,000
Completed: March 2015
Design architect: Michael D. Szerbaty, Architect
Photography: Jon Reis with Dede Hatch / Jon Reis Photography

Cornell ILR 34th Street Conference Center (p54–63)
Location: Manhattan, New York
Client: ILR Cornell University
Size: 11,000 sq ft
Cost: $1,120,000
Construction Completion: September 2008
Photography: Norman McGrath Photography

Mosaic Pre-K Center (p68–85)
Location: Queens, New York
Client: NYC School Construction Authority
Size: 33,000 sq ft
Cost: $33,000,000
Completed: August 2022
Photography: Pavel Bendov / ArchExplorer

Pre-K Center K613 (p90–99)
Location: Brooklyn, New York
Client: NYC School Construction Authority
Size: 30,000 sq ft
Cost: $27,637,000
Completed: August 2018
Photography: Jon Reis with Dede Hatch / Jon Reis Photography

NYCHA Superstorm Sandy Resiliency & Renewal Program at LaGuardia Houses (p100–107)
Location: Manhattan, New York
Client: NYC Housing Authority
Size: 10.67 acre site, Size of Electric Service Building: 2,000 sq ft
Cost: $8,700,000
Completed: May 2020
Photography: Jon Reis with Dede Hatch / Jon Reis Photography

NYCHA: Child Care and Community Center at Redfern Houses Complex (p108–19)
Location: Manhattan, New York
Client: NYC Housing Authority
Size: 10,064 sq ft
Cost: $9,000,000 (for Child Care and Community Center only)
Cost of entire Houses Complex project: $98,000,000
Completed: January 2022
Photography: Pavel Bendov / ArchExplorer

Universal Physical Education Gyms (p124–31)
Locations: Brooklyn, Queens, and the Bronx, New York
Client: NYC School Construction Authority
Size: 5,724 sq ft prototype
Cost: $7,900,000 (average for 10 projects)
Completed: November 2019 (first project PS81)
Photography: Jon Reis with Dede Hatch / Jon Reis Photography

Ocean Bay Apartment (Bayside)
Sandy Resiliency & Renewal Program (p132–45)
Location: Far Rockaways, Queens, New York
Client: NYCHA
Size: 32 acre site
Cost: $222,000,000
Construction Completion: 2019
Photography: van der Moga Photography

Early Childhood Education and the Influence of Color (the UPKs) (p146–49)

Pre-K Center 381
Location: Queens, New York
Client: NYC School Construction Authority
Size: 12,164 sq ft + Playground 3,100 sq ft
Cost: $10,000,000
Completed: September 2015

Pre-K Center 391
Location: New York, New York
Client: NYC School Construction Authority
Size: School 15,000 sq ft + entrance 839 sq ft
Cost: $9,600,000
Completed: September 2015

Pre-K Center 68
Location: Staten Island, New York
Client: NYC School Construction Authority
Size: 17,000 sq ft + Playground 3,200 sq ft
Cost: $12,000,000
Completed: September 2015
Photography: Jon Reis with Dede Hatch / Jon Reis Photography

Richard Rodgers School PS96X Addition (p150–59)
Location: Bronx, New York
Client: NYC School Construction Authority
Size: 50,266 sq ft
Cost: $40,000,000
Completed: August 2016
Photography: Jon Reis with Dede Hatch / Jon Reis Photography

Acknowledgments

The Firm

The body of work designed and constructed by MDSA builds upon a long firm history, which has always produced projects of a wide variety of building type and scale. Producing quality work with a diverse clientele, always budget-conscious, is a forte of the office. Respectful professional relationships, good communication skills, and technically precise documents allow the work to happen. Great dedication also goes into the construction phase of each project, where our architects strive to translate the vision inherent in the drawings into built form.

None of this would be possible without the core group of architects the firm employs. The architects at MDSA have a wide-ranging skill set, and are reliant on one another in support of an overall design philosophy. The people who have contributed to this continuity over the years and have been involved in the projects within this monograph are:

Michael Freedman – Partner

Since 2014 Michael has been a close design collaborator, guiding projects forward with keen oversight and stewardship. Great credit is due to him for the success of the firm's work.

Michael Speronza
Jason Campagna
Melissa Makowski
Matt Wasnewsky

None of the projects produced by the firm would be possible without their unwavering commitment and interest in doing quality work.

Photography

Enormous credit must be given to the photographers who documented the work. They were dedicated to taking the time to capture the essence of Light, Color, Texture, and Materials in the respective context.

A particular appreciation and reverence are given to Jon Reis and Dede Hatch, who were responsible for many of the images in the monograph, and have worked with the firm for many years. Constantly waiting and looking for that "magic moment," their work really made the essence of the monograph possible. Shooting with a narrow depth of field (a 100mm lens at the widest aperture), the precision of the detail and the material(s) that comprise the image give a different appreciation of the thought process in design and the ultimate achievement of the built work. Many of the images are just beautiful artwork, capturing an essence of light, materiality, texture, and color that is really what architecture is about.

Photography credits

Dede Hatch: pages 6, 9, 65 (middle, bottom right), 67 (middle, bottom right, bottom left), 89 (bottom left), 161 (top left, top right, bottom left), 163 (top left, bottom right, bottom left, middle), 169 (bottom right)

Jon Reis: pages 10, 13, 17 (middle, bottom right, bottom left), 19 (all), 65 (top left, bottom left), 67 (top right), 87 (top right, bottom left), 89 (top left, middle, bottom right), 147 (all), 149 (all), 161 (middle, bottom right), 163 (top right), 166-67, 169 (middle right, bottom left, middle left), 170-71

Pavel Bendov / ArchExplorer: pages 2-3, 14, 17 (top left, top right), 87 (top left, bottom right), 89 (top right)

Norman McGrath Photography: pages 65 (bottom left), 67 (top left)

MDSA Photography: pages 65 (top right), 169 (top left, top right)

Otto Baitz Photography: page 165 (top left, bottom left)

Steve Gottlieb Photography: page 165 (top right, bottom left)

Ryan Marshall: pages 4, 16–19 (background), 64–67 (background), 86–89 (background), 120–23 (background), 146–49 (background), 160–69 (background).

Published in Australia in 2024 by
The Images Publishing Group Pty Ltd
ABN 89 059 734 431

Offices

Melbourne
Waterman Business Centre
Suite 64, Level 2 UL40
1341 Dandenong Rd,
Chadstone, VIC 3148
Australia
Tel: +61 3 8564 8122

New York
6 West 18th Street 4B
New York City, NY 10011
United States
Tel: +1 212 645 1111

Shanghai
6F, Building C, 838 Guangji Road
Hongkou District, Shanghai 200434
China
Tel: +86 021 31260822

books@imagespublishing.com
www.imagespublishing.com

The Images Publishing Group Reference Number: 1715

All photography is attributed in the Credits on pages 172–73 and page 175.

NATIONAL LIBRARY OF AUSTRALIA
A catalogue record for this book is available from the National Library of Australia

Title: Light, Color, Texture: The Work of MDSA MDSzerbaty Associates Architecture
Author: Michael D. Szerbaty, MDSA
ISBN: 9781864709858

This title was commissioned in IMAGES' Melbourne office and produced as follows: *Editorial* Danielle Hampshire, Jeanette Wall, *Graphic design/Project management* Ryan Marshall, *Production* Nicole Boehringer

FSC www.fsc.org MIX Paper from responsible sources FSC® C019910

Printed on 140gsm Da Dong wood free paper (FSC®) by Artron Art (Group) Co., Ltd, in China

IMAGES has included on its website a page for special notices in relation to this and its other publications.
Please visit www.imagespublishing.com